D1560759

Storyteller

GALATIANS

CALLED TO BE FREE

Storyteller

GALATIANS

CALLED TO BE FREE

Lifeway Press®
Brentwood, Tennessee

Editorial Team

Cynthia Hopkins
Writer

Angel Prohaska
Associate Editor

Stephanie Cross
Associate Editor

Jon Rodda
Art Director

Reid Patton
Senior Editor

Tyler Quillet
Managing Editor

Joel Polk
Publisher, Small Group Publishing

John Paul Basham
Director, Adult Ministry Publishing

© 2023 Lifeway Press®

No part of this book may be reproduced or transmitted in any form or by any means, electronic or mechanical, including photocopying and recording, or by any information storage or retrieval system, except as may be expressly permitted in writing by the publisher. Requests for permission should be addressed in writing to Lifeway Press®; 200 Powell Place, Suite 100, Brentwood, TN 37027-7707.

ISBN: 978-1-4300-8484-6 • Item number: 005845999
Dewey decimal classification: 227.4 • Subject heading: BIBLE / EPISTLES / GALATIANS

All Scripture quotations are taken from the Christian Standard Bible®, Copyright © 2017 by Holman Bible Publishers. Used by permission. Christian Standard Bible® and CSB® are federally registered trademarks of Holman Bible Publishers.

To order additional copies of this resource, write to Lifeway Resources Customer Service; 200 Powell Place, Suite 100, Brentwood, TN 27027-7707; fax 615-251-5933; call toll free 800-458-2772; order online at Lifeway.com; or email orderentry@lifeway.com.

Printed in the United States of America

Adult Ministry Publishing • Lifeway Resources • 200 Powell Place • Brentwood, TN 37027-7707

CONTENTS

THE STORYTELLER SERIES

God could've chosen to reveal Himself in any way that He desired, yet in His wisdom, He chose to reveal Himself in the context of a story. We come to know and understand this reality as we immerse ourselves in the Scriptures and begin to see the entirety of Scripture as one interconnected story. By becoming familiar with the individual stories of Scripture, we train ourselves to see each as one part of God's big story.

Storyteller is a series of devotional and group Bible study experiences designed to take people through Scripture in a way that is beautiful, intuitive, and interactive. Each volume uses a book of the Bible or a portion of Scripture from within a book to examine a key theme. This theme guides the Bible study experience and gives readers handles to help understand and digest what they're reading.

At the end of each study, your should have a deeper understanding of God, His Word, the big themes of Scripture, the connectedness of God's story, and His work in your life.

Let's enter the story together.

ABOUT GALATIANS

AUTHOR

The apostle Paul is the author of the letter to the Galatians. This view is rarely disputed. In the first three words, Paul identifies himself as the author, and everything that follows is consistent with what we know about his life and theology from other New Testament writings.

Paul was a highly educated Jewish Pharisee and Roman citizen who was dramatically converted to Christianity in AD 35. Chosen by God to proclaim the name of Jesus to Jews and Gentiles alike, Paul lived the rest of his days faithfully carrying out that purpose.

BACKGROUND

Because the term "Galatians" was used both politically and ethnically, the exact location of churches to which Galatians was written is less certain than its authorship. Most likely, however, Paul wrote to the churches in southern Galatia that he had helped plant on his first missionary journey. This included the cities Pisidian Antioch, Iconium, Lystra, and Derbe (Acts 13:14–14:23). Paul had received word that these churches were now being taught—and had begun to accept—a false gospel.

DATE

Galatians was written sometime between AD 48 and AD 56, depending largely on the view one takes of the location of its original audience. However, because the book's contents address the same topic discussed at the Jerusalem Council in AD 49 (Acts 15), yet does not mention that meeting or its conclusions, it is likely that Paul wrote Galatians in AD 48 or 49 before the Jerusalem Council had occurred. This view dates Galatians as one of the earliest New Testament books.

PURPOSE

After Paul had started churches in Galatia, he got word that false teachers had come behind him to undermine the gospel message and Paul's apostleship. These Judaizers insisted that Gentile converts must be circumcised. They taught that to live in the freedom of grace was, in fact, lawless and sinful. Understanding the essential nature of the matter, Paul wrote to clarify and defend the gospel of grace. Paul wanted the Galatians to know they were justified and empowered to live in holiness by Christ alone—not by any works of the law.

WHY STUDY GALATIANS?

The human need for spiritual correction happens fast and often.

Less than two decades after Jesus died and resurrected, the apostle Paul wrote Galatians to Christians who were beginning to think they had something to do with their own salvation.

In 1517, Martin Luther's study of Galatians prompted him to write 95 theses on a piece of paper and nail it to a church door in Germany. He wanted to get the attention of Christians in his day who also thought they had something to do with their own salvation.

Reformation was needed, and so that continues today. The specific applications that demonstrate our wrong understanding change, but the reason for them stays the same— we are often tempted to think we have something to do with our salvation.

Even when we say we believe we are saved by grace, our faith practice often shows a different view.

We make certain religious practices necessary for salvation, determine to continue in our salvation through self-effort, or believe it is up to our own ability to enact spiritual change in other people. These, and more, are false gospels that need correction.

In 1674, Jodocus van Lodenstein put it like this: "*ecclesia reformata, semper reformanda secundum verbi Dei* (the church is reformed, and is always [in need of] being according to the Word of God)."[1] The same is true for each individual believer in Christ.

And the message of Galatians is where reformation always begins.

---

1. R. Scott Clark and Joel E. Kim, eds., *Always Reformed: Essays in Honor of W. Robert Godfrey* (Escondido, CA: Westminster Seminary California, 2012), 116-134, quoted in Kevin DeYoung, "Semper Reformanda," The Gospel Coalition, October 27, 2016, www.thegospelcoalition.org/blogs/kevin-deyoung/ semper-reformanda/.

OUTLINE OF GALATIANS

I. The Imperative of Grace (1:1-9)

II. The Authenticity of the Gospel Message (1:10–2:21)

III. The Way of Salvation (3:1–4:31)

IV. The Implications of Freedom (5:1–6:10)

V. The Effect of the Cross (6:11-18)

HOW TO USE THIS STUDY

Each week follows a repeated rhythm to guide you in your study of Galatians and was crafted with lots of white space and photographic imagery to facilitate a time of reflection on Scripture.

The week begins with an introduction to the themes of the week. Throughout each week you'll find Scripture readings, devotions, and beautiful imagery to guide your time.

WEEK 6

FREE TO DO GOOD

<table>
<tr><td>DAY
1</td><td>RESCUE STORY</td></tr>
</table>

Paul typically began his New Testament letters with words of affirmation for his audience. He told the Romans they were "loved by God, called as saints." The Corinthians were "sanctified in Christ Jesus." The Ephesians were "faithful saints." And he called the Colossians "faithful brothers and sisters."

The Galatians received no such pat on the back.

Because they questioned the most essential teaching they'd received, Paul got straight to the point. He outlined his authority and cut to the chase.

The appeal to his authority as an apostle is essential to the contents of the letter. An apostle is someone sent by God to exercise a specific kind of leadership in the New Testament church. Like the other apostles, the resurrected Jesus Christ appeared to Paul and called him to the role of apostle. The gospel message is their message—salvation comes from Jesus alone.

The gospel message Paul taught brings the grace and peace that Jesus offered and we all desire. In fact, we can't experience those blessings any other way.

The good news of the gospel begins with grace—the unmerited favor of God—given to us by His Son, Jesus. Peace is the implication of that grace. On our very best day, sin utterly defeats us. In our own ability, power, and ingenuity, we have no hope of rescue—ever. But we do have hope.

Jesus died in our place to rescue us.

The grace that rescues us from death gives us the peace of new life. We can't earn our way to God—to try to is an exhausting pursuit. But Jesus provides another way. God came to us to call us to the kind of freedom that only He can offer. This is good news, for the Galatians and for us.

GALATIANS 1:1-5

GREETING

1 Paul, an apostle — not from men or by man, but by Jesus Christ and God the Father who raised him from the dead — ² and all the brothers who are with me:

To the churches of Galatia.

³ Grace to you and peace from God the Father and our Lord Jesus Christ, ⁴ who gave himself for our sins to rescue us from this present evil age, according to the will of our God and Father. ⁵ To him be the glory forever and ever. Amen.

Each week includes five days of Scripture reading along with a short devotional thought and three questions to process what you've read.

The Scripture reading is printed out for you with plenty of space for you to take notes, circle, underline, and interact with the passage.

For freedom, Christ set us free. Stand firm, then,
and don't submit again to a yoke of slavery.
GALATIANS 5:1

The sixth day contains no reading beyond a couple of verses to give you time to pause and listen to what God has said through the Scriptures this week. You may be tempted to skip this day all together, but resist this temptation. Sit and be quiet with God—even if it's only for a few minutes.

The seventh day each week offers a list of open-ended questions that apply to any passage of Scripture. Use this day to reflect on your own or meet with a group to discuss what you've learned. Take intentional time to remember and reflect on what the story of Galatians is teaching you.

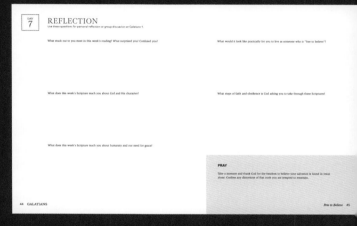

What stuck out to you most in this week's reading? What surprised you? Confused you?

What would it look like practically for you to live as someone who is "free to believe"?

What does this week's Scripture teach you about God and His character?

What steps of faith and obedience is God asking you to take through these Scriptures?

What does this week's Scripture teach you about humanity and our need for grace?

PRAY

Take a moment and thank God for the freedom to believe your salvation is found in Jesus alone. Confess any distortions of that truth you are tempted to entertain.

Know your
IDENTITY

An allegory is a spiritual or symbolic interpretation of a story that also has a literal meaning. In Galatians 4:21-31 Paul uses allegory to present the truth about Christian identity—we are children of promise. Consider what these other Bible passages that use allegory and metaphor teach us about our identity in Christ.

 You are a new creation.
2 CORINTHIANS 5:17

 You are God's temple.
1 CORINTHIANS 6:19–20

 You are loved and forgiven by your Father.
LUKE 15:11–32

 You are good soil, producing a good crop.
MATTHEW 13:3–9

 You are the bride of Christ.
EPHESIANS 5:21–32

 You are wholly dependent on Christ.
JOHN 15:1–8

 You are a conqueror.
ROMANS 8:37

 You are the light of the world.
MATTHEW 5:14–16

Throughout each week of study, you will notice callout boxes or supplemental pages provided to give greater context and clarity to the Scripture you're reading. These features will help you connect the story of Galatians to the bigger story of Scripture.

LEADING A GROUP

Each week of study contains a set of questions that can be used for small group meetings. These open-ended questions are meant to guide discussion of the week's Scripture passage. No matter the size of your group, here are some helpful tips for guiding discussion.

PREPARE

REVIEW the Scripture and your answers to the week's questions ahead of time.

PRAY over your group as well as the Scriptures you've been studying. Ask God's Spirit for help to lead the group deeper into God's truth and deeper in relationship with one another.

MINIMIZE DISTRACTIONS

We live in a time when our attention is increasingly divided. Try to see your group time as a space and respite from the digital clutter—from scrolling, notifications, likes, and newsfeeds. Commit to one another to give focused time and attention to the discussion at hand and minimize outside distractions. Help people focus on what's most important: connecting with God, with the Bible, and with one another.

ENCOURAGE DISCUSSION

A good small group experience has the following characteristics.

EVERYONE IS INCLUDED. Your goal is to foster a community where people are welcome just as they are but encouraged to grow spiritually.

EVERYONE PARTICIPATES. Encourage everyone to ask questions, share, or read aloud.

NO ONE DOMINATES. Even though you may be "leading" the group, try to see yourself as a participant steering the conversation rather than a teacher imparting information.

DON'T RUSH. Don't feel that a moment of silence is a bad thing. People may need time, and we should be glad to give it to them. Don't feel like you have to ask all the questions or stay away from questions that aren't included. Be sensitive to the Holy Spirit and to one another. Take your time.

INPUT IS AFFIRMED AND FOLLOWED UP. Make sure you point out something true or helpful in a response. Don't just move on. Build community with follow-up questions, asking other people to share when they have experienced similar things or how a truth has shaped their understanding of God and the Scripture you're studying. Conversation stalls when people feel that you don't want to hear their answers or that you're looking for only a certain answer. Engagement and affirmation keeps the conversation going.

GOD AND HIS WORD ARE CENTRAL. The questions in this study are meant to steer the conversation back to God, His Word, and the work of the gospel in our lives. Opinions and experiences are valuable and can be helpful, but God is the center of the Bible, the center of our story, and should be the center of our discussion. Trust Him to lead the discussion. Continually point people to the Word and to active steps of faith.

KEEP CONNECTING

Spiritual growth occurs in the context of community. Think of ways to connect with group members during the week. Your group will be more enjoyable the more you get to know one another through time spent outside of an official group meeting. The more people are comfortable with and involved in one another's lives, the more they'll look forward to being together. When people move beyond being friendly to truly being friends who form a community, they come to each session eager to engage instead of merely attending. Reserve time each week to touch base with individual group members.

WEEK 1

FREE TO BELIEVE

No other "gospel" saves.

The best books hook you from page one.

Maybe that's why many people consider Galatians a favorite among books of the Bible. Only a few sentences into the letter, the intensity becomes clear. The same issue and intensity resonates now, more than two thousand years later.

What we know and read today as the book of Galatians is a preserved letter written by the apostle Paul to the church in Galatia, a region in the Roman province of Asia which included the cities Pisidian Antioch, Iconium, Lystra, and Derbe. The Christians in this region faced struggles Christians endure today too.

The believers in Galatia were free to believe they were loved and redeemed by God by grace alone through faith in Jesus Christ. *So are we*. But they struggled to fully embrace that freedom. *So do we*. Prominent voices inside and outside the church were teaching contrary to the freedom found in Jesus. *Voices like these are so prolific today that sometimes we don't even recognize them.*

The apostle Paul caught wind of the opposing view, and he was moved to respond with force to remind the Galatians of the freedom they had in Jesus. So begins chapter 1 of his six chapter defense of the gospel of grace.

The truths presented offer an equally profound effect for every person's life today.

They are, in fact, a matter of life and death.

We're surrounded by different "gospels." And God calls us daily to turn them all aside to freely believe in the only gospel that saves—the gospel of grace.

GALATIANS 1:1-5

1 Paul, an apostle — not from men or by man, but by Jesus Christ and God the Father who raised him from the dead — ² and all the brothers who are with me:

To the churches of Galatia.

³ Grace to you and peace from God the Father and our Lord Jesus Christ, ⁴ who gave himself for our sins to rescue us from this present evil age, according to the will of our God and Father. ⁵ To him be the glory forever and ever. Amen.

<table>
<tr><td>DAY
1</td><td></td></tr>
</table>

RESCUE STORY

Paul typically began his New Testament letters with words of affirmation for his audience. He told the Romans they were "loved by God, called as saints." The Corinthians were "sanctified in Christ Jesus." The Ephesians were "faithful saints." And he called the Colossians "faithful brothers and sisters."

The Galatians received no such pat on the back.

Because they questioned the most essential teaching they'd received, Paul got straight to the point. He outlined his authority and cut to the chase.

The appeal to his authority as an apostle is essential to the contents of the letter. An apostle is someone sent by God to exercise a specific kind of leadership in the New Testament church. Like the other apostles, the resurrected Jesus Christ appeared to Paul and called him to the role of apostle. The gospel message is their message—salvation comes from Jesus alone.

The gospel message Paul taught brings the grace and peace that Jesus offered and we all desire. In fact, we can't experience those blessings any other way.

The good news of the gospel begins with grace—the unmerited favor of God—given to us by His Son, Jesus. Peace is the implication of that grace. On our very best day, sin utterly defeats us. In our own ability, power, and ingenuity, we have no hope of rescue—ever. But we do have hope.

Jesus died in our place to rescue us.

The grace that rescues us from death gives us the peace of new life. We can't earn our way to God—to try to is an exhausting pursuit. But Jesus provides another way. God came to us to call us to the kind of freedom that only He can offer. This is good news, for the Galatians and for us.

The only way to experience peace is in relationship with Jesus.

REFLECTIONS

What do we learn about God in these five short verses?

In His sovereignty, God has now made you the recipient of Paul's letter to the Galatians. What message does He want you to hear in these first five verses?

How would you counsel someone who is struggling to find peace?

TRACING THE STORY

The New Testament writers paired grace and peace in their letters as an introductory greeting seventeen times. The majority of those are followed by the words "from God our Father and the Lord Jesus Christ." In the Old Testament, Isaiah 54:10 and other passages refer to God's promise of spiritual freedom as the "covenant of peace." Galatians echoes the overarching message of Scripture—in an act of pure grace, God sent His Son Jesus to free humanity from the bondage of sin and restore our peace with Him.

GALATIANS 1:6-10

NO OTHER GOSPEL

⁶ I am amazed that you are so quickly turning away from him who called you by the grace of Christ and are turning to a different gospel — ⁷ not that there is another gospel, but there are some who are troubling you and want to distort the gospel of Christ. ⁸ But even if we or an angel from heaven should preach to you a gospel contrary to what we have preached to you, a curse be on him! ⁹ As we have said before, I now say again: If anyone is preaching to you a gospel contrary to what you received, a curse be on him!

¹⁰ For am I now trying to persuade people, or God? Or am I striving to please people? If I were still trying to please people, I would not be a servant of Christ.

DAY	
2	

TRUE STORY

Finish the following sentence: I am amazed that some people who claim to believe in Jesus _____.

We are all sinners saved by grace and seeking to step forward in the peace that grace brings. At the same time, we have expectations of ourselves and other Christians. If those expectations are founded in the grace and peace of Christ, we don't need to apologize for them. The New Testament writers certainly didn't.

To say the gospel comes to us by grace through faith in Jesus Christ simply means the gospel comes to us as an unearned gift from God (by grace) because of our belief and trust in the life, death, and resurrection of Jesus (through faith in Jesus Christ). The real gospel is no more and no less than this. Any "gospel" that adds to or takes away from this is no gospel at all.

The opening of the letter finds Paul amazed, and not in a good way. Not long after leaving Galatia, the church in that region turned to false teaching. They began listening to teachers who gave a message that conflicted with the gospel of grace. This "different gospel" added requirements of the Jewish ceremonial law to salvation.

Paul didn't water down what was happening. This was serious business, made clear when he used the word *cursed* to describe those who participated. Any teaching that is contrary to salvation by grace alone through faith in Jesus Christ is wrong— even if that teaching is given by the most eloquent, persuasive, impressive, and intelligent person you've ever met.

There are terrible consequences for every person who accepts a false gospel (Hebrews 2:1-4). Whether we add rules Jesus never intended or water down the truth to suit cultural norms of behavior, we are missing the richness that can only be found in the only gospel that saves.

Any teaching that is contrary to the gospel is wrong—and has no power to save.

REFLECTIONS

In your own words, what did Paul mean by, "If I were still trying to please people, I would not be a servant of Christ" (v. 10)?

Based on Galatians 1:6-10, what would it look like for you to please God and serve Christ this week?

What does it mean, practically, to "distort the gospel of Christ" (v. 7)? How can you avoid it?

Turning Away

We always have and always will have the freedom to believe.
And we always have and always will be tempted toward unbelief.

GALATIANS 1:6-8

[6] I am amazed that you are so quickly turning away from
him who called you by the grace of Christ and are turning to
a different gospel — [7] not that there is another gospel, but
there are some who are troubling you and want to distort
the gospel of Christ. [8] But even if we or an angel from heaven
should preach to you a gospel contrary to what we have
preached to you, a curse be on him!

PROVERBS 14:12

[12] There is a way that seems right to a person,
but its end is the way to death.

Adam and Eve...

... turned from God's loving instruction to the serpent's cunning deceit.
GENESIS 3:1-8V

Israel...

... turned from God's future promise to their oppressive past.
NUMBERS 14:4

... turned from worship of God to the worship of worthless idols.
JEREMIAH 2:5-7

... turned from God's voice and shut their ears so they could not hear.
ZECHARIAH 7:8-12

David...

... turned from his pursuit of God's heart to his own selfish desires.
2 SAMUEL 11

Many disciples...

... turned from Jesus and no longer followed Him.
JOHN 6:66

Peter...

... turned from Jesus to fear and self-preservation.
LUKE 22:55-62

Some people...

... will turn from faith to deceitful, demonic teachings.
1 TIMOTHY 4:1-2

Many people...

... will turn from the truth to what they want to hear.
2 TIMOTHY 4:3-4

All people...

... can turn back to God in repentance and be restored in Jesus Christ.
ACTS 3:19-21

GALATIANS 1:11-12

THE ORIGIN OF PAUL'S GOSPEL

[11] For I want you to know, brothers and sisters, that the gospel preached by me is not of human origin. [12] For I did not receive it from a human source and I was not taught it, but it came by a revelation of Jesus Christ.

ORIGIN STORY

Change is a constant in life.

People grow. Technological advancement changes our rhythms of life. Words and vernacular shift in meaning. Trends and fashions come in and out of style then back into style again.

But the gospel isn't like that.

The Galatians had heard Paul's message and then right behind him came a different teaching. More than confusing, it was dangerous. Paul wanted them to know the gospel doesn't evolve into new, better strategies. The gospel doesn't have a human origin, so it doesn't need human reinvention. It came directly from God.

This was, and is, an important statement of fact. Some people were preaching a false gospel. The Galatians could know it was false because it came from the teachers and circumstances around them. In other words, it had a worldly origin.

The message Paul preached wasn't something he or anyone else had made up. He hadn't learned it from a trendy philosopher of his time. He hadn't gleaned it from the lyrics of a popular song. No church group had formulated the plan. Paul hadn't even learned it in a seminary class. Instead, he received the gospel directly from Jesus Christ.

The message Paul taught was different from the message from the teachers who came behind him. They were legalists, because they wanted to add to the law. The gospel differs from any human message in character and content because it has a divine origin.

We are free to believe the gospel message because it comes to us from God and He gives it freely. What He defines, we don't get to redefine. If we do, we're wrong.

You are free to believe the gospel
message because the gospel message
originates with the eternal God.

REFLECTIONS

Why was it important for the Galatians to know the gospel message came from God?

Why does the gospel's origin give us freedom to believe it?

What "new" messages from the world tempt you to divert your attention from the true gospel? How can you guard against giving into that temptation?

TRACING THE STORY
Jesus was with God in the beginning, and Jesus is the Word of God (John 1:1-2,14). From the beginning, God began to reveal the gospel message (Genesis 3:15; 12:1-3; 17:6-8). Jesus, who was with God in the beginning, is the fulfillment of the law. God's plan to redeem people from their sin and separation from Him is fulfilled, once and for all time, in the life, death, and resurrection of Jesus (Romans 8:3-4).

GALATIANS 1:13-17

[13] For you have heard about my former way of life in Judaism: I intensely persecuted God's church and tried to destroy it. [14] I advanced in Judaism beyond many contemporaries among my people, because I was extremely zealous for the traditions of my ancestors. [15] But when God, who from my mother's womb set me apart and called me by his grace, was pleased [16] to reveal his Son in me, so that I could preach him among the Gentiles, I did not immediately consult with anyone. [17] I did not go up to Jerusalem to those who had become apostles before me; instead I went to Arabia and came back to Damascus.

PERSONAL STORY

Paul probably wished he had a different story. It couldn't have been easy to recount the horrific acts he had previously committed against Christians. But we see here in Galatians, in Paul's other letters, and in Acts that he shared his story again and again.

Why would he choose to publicly revisit the greatest regret of his life? Why would he risk the emotional vulnerability such transparency would invite? Why would anyone?

Paul shared his story in its truest, ugliest form, because his story was a clear picture of the power of the gospel and the change Christ brings. The gospel freed Paul from a bad story and replaced it with a better story.

By grace, God reached into Paul's destructive heart and set him on the path of life. By grace, God called Paul out of darkness, revealed Jesus to him, and set him apart. As such, Paul's story didn't end in ugliness. It became a beautiful and powerful story. The gospel changed Paul's life, and he fought to keep that message clear and available to all.

Every Christian's story is one of grace and power; it's the story of abandoning the shackles of sin for the boundless hope of freedom with Jesus.

The gospel is a God-inspired story, and it is also every Christian's personal story. That's true whether you are the greatest missionary the world has ever known or a new convert in Galatia where different teachings confuse your understanding. It's true whether you grew up going to church every week or rejecting God entirely. None of us are the sum of our choices; we are the products of Jesus's care for us.

We are free to believe the gospel because the gospel story has the power to change our story. In this sense, we all have the same story—and each story reveals beautiful evidence of the power of God's amazing grace.

Every salvation story reveals
the power of God's grace.

REFLECTIONS

What does Paul's story teach you about the power of God's grace in Christ?

What is your faith story? How did your need for grace show up in your life? Through what circumstances did God's plan, power, and beauty demonstrate themselves in your life?

Is it difficult for you to share your story of faith? What benefit would other people gain from hearing it?

GALATIANS 1:18-24

[18] Then after three years I did go up to Jerusalem to get to know Cephas, and I stayed with him fifteen days. [19] But I didn't see any of the other apostles except James, the Lord's brother. [20] I declare in the sight of God: I am not lying in what I write to you.

[21] Afterward, I went to the regions of Syria and Cilicia. [22] I remained personally unknown to the Judean churches that are in Christ. [23] They simply kept hearing, "He who formerly persecuted us now preaches the faith he once tried to destroy." [24] And they glorified God because of me.

POLARIZING STORY

These days, if we want a message to gain traction, we must build a platform—grow a social media following, host a podcast, connect with noteworthy people, or write a book. To disappear for three years of solitude and then spend a couple of weeks with one notably outspoken person would surely cause the opposite effect.

But that's exactly what Paul did. His personal story didn't include building a name for himself by rubbing elbows with Galatia's annual list of the most influential people. Instead, he'd avoided everyone for three years. Then he spent fifteen days with Peter (called Cephas in this passage) and shook hands once or twice with James before heading back into a place where he was largely unknown.

Paul explained this to the Galatian churches to help them understand the validity of his teaching. Paul's teaching came to Him from Jesus, not the apostles, yet it was unified with the gospel message the apostles preached. In his days as a Jewish teacher and leader, Paul was known for his strict adherence to the Jewish law and his zealous persecution of Christians. He built that name for himself through years of effort.

The gospel gave Paul the freedom to stop building a name for himself and to learn about Jesus and build his new faith in obscurity. His new belief in Jesus cost him his platform and threatened his life.

While Paul enjoyed those brief moments with Peter and James, he learned of a plot against his life (Acts 9:29). Opposition to the gospel had come quickly. The incredible change that had taken place in his life was spreading. He had gone from persecutor to preacher, and people responded in different ways. Some praised God; others plotted his death.

The gospel was polarizing in Paul's day, and it is polarizing now. But it is also freeing. It frees us from platform and frees us from who others expect us to be. And it frees us to glorify God in the way that He has called us to.

You must choose to believe
the gospel of grace.

REFLECTIONS

After converting to Christianity, why would Paul have spent three years alone with the Lord?

What does Paul's personal process of learning teach you about your role in spiritual growth and the freedom to believe?

Paul went from persecutor to preacher. What about you? Name one change that has taken place in your life since you chose to believe the gospel of grace in Jesus Christ. What has the gospel freed you from?

PAUSE & LISTEN

Spend some time reflecting over the week's reading.

For I want you to know, brothers and sisters, that the gospel preached by me is not of human origin. For I did not receive it from a human source and I was not taught it, but it came by a revelation of Jesus Christ.

REFLECTION
Use these questions for personal reflection or group discussion on Galatians 1.

What stuck out to you most in this week's reading? What surprised you? Confused you?

What does this week's Scripture teach you about God and His character?

What does this week's Scripture teach you about humanity and our need for grace?

What would it look like practically for you to live as someone who is "free to believe"?

What steps of faith and obedience is God asking you to take through these Scriptures?

PRAY

Take a moment and thank God for the freedom to believe your salvation is found in Jesus alone. Confess any distortions of that truth you are tempted to entertain.

WEEK 2

FREE TO
CONTEND

Grace is essential.

Most of us want to avoid conflict.

What we see on the internet and other media these days might make that fact seem less obvious, but even public disputes we experience only as spectators often make us uncomfortable—and prove the point.

Conflict avoidance might make life easier, but what's easiest might not always be best. We have to consider, *What is at stake?* Some conflicts are worth having.

Minimizing the grace in the gospel of grace is one of those conflicts worth having.

Grace is essential. To add works, striving, and effort to the gospel is to make it no gospel at all. Paul couldn't look the other way as false teachers manipulated the gospel and added burden where God gave freedom.

If Paul had avoided the hard conversation, this teaching that was leading people away from freedom and to an eternity separated from God would've continued.

The message of salvation by grace through faith in Jesus alone was worth the fight. It still is. The freedom we've found from sin and shame is worth sharing. It's worth believing. It's worth contending for.

Essential matters of the faith are just that—*essential.*

GALATIANS 2:1-2

PAUL DEFENDS HIS GOSPEL AT JERUSALEM

2 Then after fourteen years I went up again to Jerusalem with Barnabas, taking Titus along also. ² I went up according to a revelation and presented to them the gospel I preach among the Gentiles, but privately to those recognized as leaders. I wanted to be sure I was not running, and had not been running, in vain.

DAY 8 | FOR ACCOUNTABILITY

Shifting into chapter 2, Paul moved on from discussing the source of the gospel to discussing the nature of the gospel.

The purity of the gospel message was so important that Paul had gone to Jerusalem to sort it out. His intention wasn't to stir up conflict but to bring resolution to the conflict that existed. Paul's passion for gospel clarity wasn't abstract; he had already had this debate in Jerusalem.

He didn't prop himself up and diminish others—he brought unity by clarifying the mission of the church.

And that's what happened! When he submitted himself to the leadership of the church in Jerusalem, God confirmed to them all that neither culture, tradition, nor personal opinion can change the gospel.

Paul's willingness to engage in the discussion invited accountability for him and everyone else. In going to the leaders in Jerusalem, he modeled both humility and submission. He hoped the Galatians would respond to his letter similarly.

Would they? More importantly, will we?

To be truly free to rightly contend for the pure gospel message, we must readily submit ourselves to examination.

We need to ask specific questions of ourselves and others: Is our culture shaping our views? Are our beliefs shaped more by the way we do things or by Scripture? Are long-held traditions or personal opinions causing us to add rules to God's free gift of grace?

Or, by God's grace, through the accountability of His Word and in community with other Christians, are we confidently rejecting false teaching so that the pure, joyful message of Jesus's finished work on the cross will be spread across the globe?

You need the accountability of God's Word and the community of faith to rightly contend for the gospel.

REFLECTIONS

Why did Paul make the trip to Jerusalem to visit the church leaders?

Have you ever wondered if your service to the Lord is an exercise in vanity? Based on Galatians 2:1-2, what should you do when that happens?

Are you willing to receive correction concerning your beliefs? If so, what do you do to invite it? If not, why not? How might refusing correction be dangerous?

INSIGHTS

We can't be certain whether the visit to Jerusalem Paul described in Galatians 2:1 was the visit recorded in Acts 11:30, where Paul and Barnabas took famine relief to the church in Jerusalem, or the visit recored in Acts 15:2 for the Jerusalem Council. Either way, the conflict in Galatia mirrors the conflict discussed in Acts 15, showing the unity of the early church against this kind of legalistic teaching that subverts the purity of the gospel.

GALATIANS 2:3-5

[3] But not even Titus, who was with me, was compelled to be circumcised, even though he was a Greek. [4] This matter arose because some false brothers had infiltrated our ranks to spy on the freedom we have in Christ Jesus in order to enslave us. [5] But we did not give up and submit to these people for even a moment, so that the truth of the gospel would be preserved for you.

FOR TRUTH

It might be valuable to be more specific about the controversy plaguing the Galatian church. As we touched on last week, a group of false teachers known as Judaizers had infiltrated the Galatian church. They argued that new Christians should follow Jewish ceremonial law, beginning with circumcision because it was the covenant God gave to Abraham (Genesis 17).

However, when this controversy was brought before the leaders of the church, they all agreed that circumcision was not required for Gentile converts. Though Titus, a Gentile, was present, they all agreed he did not need to be circumcised.

The entry point for all people into a covenant with God is the truth about Jesus Christ, not adherence to religious rituals. The truth of the gospel is that God provided Jesus as a sacrifice for our sin and all who turn from their sin and believe in Jesus's work on the cross and resurrection from the dead may have life and freedom in Jesus's name.

Jesus's sacrifice freed us from following the law. The gospel freed Gentile converts from a burden that had proven too great for the Jews to bear (Acts 15:10). The gospel only requires repentance and faith.

Paul contended that the truths of the gospel applied to all people—both Jew and Gentile—equally. The gospel frees us all from the law and places no additional burden on belief except for repentance and faith.

There is only one gospel. We must not give up or submit to any lesser truth for even a moment. To do so doesn't bring the church together at all—it only tears it apart.

The truth of the gospel unites us at the foot of the cross.

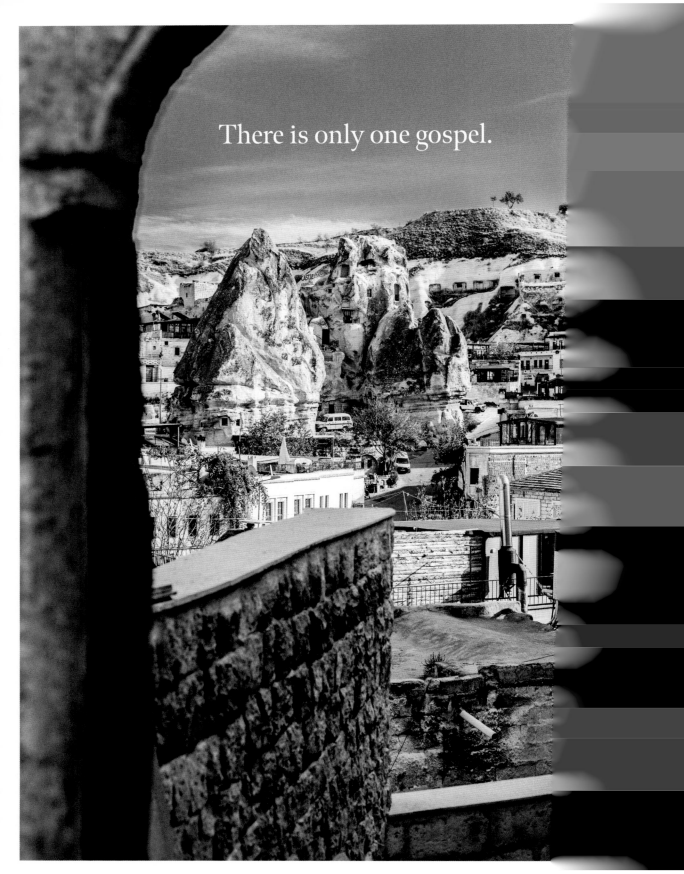

There is only one gospel.

REFLECTIONS

Why did Paul refuse to give in to the Judaizers on the issue of circumcision (v. 5)?

What pressures from culture and church push us to give in to a false gospel?

What do your actions show that you believe about salvation?

CONFLICT
and
CONFRONTATION

Paul didn't avoid conflict. He was a straight-talker, seemingly unafraid to do what he believed was good and right. Before his salvation, that meant saying (and doing) whatever was necessary to stop the gospel message. After, it meant saying and doing whatever was needed to spread the gospel message. The danger for us is that we might wrongly interpret his candor simply as a personality trait. It wasn't. The whole counsel of God's Word lets us know that God's people are called to contend for the gospel.

Consider reading the following passages to discover some questions to ask yourself so that you might contend rightly, regardless of your natural inclination.

Identify your motive.

JUDE 1:3 AND JAMES 4:1

Are you contending for the faith or for your own selfish desires?

Let God judge other's motives.

PHILIPPIANS 1:18

Are you contending in a spirit of grateful partnership or prideful criticism?

Check your attitude.

LEVITICUS 19:17-18 AND EPHESIANS 4:15-16

Are you contending in love for others or in animosity toward them?

Understand the problem.

2 TIMOTHY 3:16 AND 2 TIMOTHY 4:2-4

Are you contending in the truth of God's Word or in the leanings of popular culture?

Choose right purpose.

MATTHEW 5:9 AND ROMANS 16:17

Are you contending to bring unity and peace or to bring division?

Focus on what matters.

GALATIANS 6:15

Are you contending for spiritual transformation or to uphold a preferred tradition?

GALATIANS 2:6-10

[6] Now from those recognized as important (what they once were makes no difference to me; God does not show favoritism) — they added nothing to me. [7] On the contrary, they saw that I had been entrusted with the gospel for the uncircumcised, just as Peter was for the circumcised, [8] since the one at work in Peter for an apostleship to the circumcised was also at work in me for the Gentiles. [9] When James, Cephas, and John — those recognized as pillars — acknowledged the grace that had been given to me, they gave the right hand of fellowship to me and Barnabas, agreeing that we should go to the Gentiles and they to the circumcised. [10] They asked only that we would remember the poor, which I had made every effort to do.

FOR FELLOWSHIP

It's easier to accept that the gospel is for everyone in theory than in practice.

In practice, we divide ourselves. That's because things like differences in age, gender, ethnicity, personality traits, nationality, and language often pose questions and difficulties that take work to solve.

Fellowship—genuine friendship and community—typically happens within much smaller circles that don't require such work.

By its very nature, though, truth brings us into community. As we apply the gospel to our lives, it should unite what other lesser differences have divided. The gospel is for everyone.

That is what Paul expresses to us here. Peter, James, and John were operating primarily within a smaller circle of Jewish Christians. Paul once lived in the tight-knit circle of the Pharisees, but he believed the gospel and the gospel took two smaller circles and made them one.

Similarly the gospel compelled Peter, James, and John to go to the Jews (the circumcised in this passage), and Paul and Barnabas to the Gentiles. Gospel wisdom and faithful obedience sent these men to different circles but united them all in the larger circle of gospel fellowship.

This same practical application of grace extends to us today. God calls His people to share the gospel in numerous contexts and to live out that calling in numerous ways. Yet the gospel message is the same every time—regardless of age, gender, ethnicity, personality traits, nationality, language, or anything else. All our many circles exist together on the same gospel foundation.

This truth must not exist only in theory; it requires practical application. The unity of the gospel demands that our circles join together and take part in the community the gospel creates.

The gospel unites what lesser
differences have divided.

REFLECTIONS

How did James, Peter, and John respond to Paul and the work he was doing?

Why did Paul have fellowship with these men but not the Judaizers? What was the difference?

What differences make it difficult for you to sense unity of fellowship with other Christians? How does this passage speak to you about that?

INSIGHTS

Shaking the right hand was a sign of friendship and trust, and "fellowship" translates from the Greek word *koinonia*, which means "association," "fellowship," or "close relationship" (v. 9).[1] There is no greater partnership—in association or purpose—than spreading the gospel to unbelievers in every circle that exists. "The right hand of fellowship" is a trust worth fighting for.

1. Max Anders, *Galatians-Colossians*, vol. 8, Holman New Testament Commentary (Nashville, TN: Broadman & Holman Publishers, 1999), 27.

GALATIANS 2:11-18

FREEDOM FROM THE LAW

[11] But when Cephas came to Antioch, I opposed him to his face because he stood condemned. [12] For he regularly ate with the Gentiles before certain men came from James. However, when they came, he withdrew and separated himself, because he feared those from the circumcision party. [13] Then the rest of the Jews joined his hypocrisy, so that even Barnabas was led astray by their hypocrisy. [14] But when I saw that they were deviating from the truth of the gospel, I told Cephas in front of everyone, "If you, who are a Jew, live like a Gentile and not like a Jew, how can you compel Gentiles to live like Jews?"

[15] We are Jews by birth and not "Gentile sinners," [16] and yet because we know that a person is not justified by the works of the law but by faith in Jesus Christ, even we ourselves have believed in Christ Jesus. This was so that we might be justified by faith in Christ and not by the works of the law, because by the works of the law no human being will be justified. [17] But if we ourselves are also found to be "sinners" while seeking to be justified by Christ, is Christ then a promoter of sin? Absolutely not! [18] If I rebuild those things that I tore down, I show myself to be a lawbreaker.

FOR CORRECTION

This face-off between Paul and Peter had to be one of those situations where staying and watching feels awkward, but you just can't make yourself look away. Two influential leaders in the early church had to have an uncomfortable conversation.

As uncomfortable as it may have been, this confrontation was necessary and good.

Circumcision wasn't the only issue confronting the purity of the gospel message. There were dietary laws, too. Peter had come to terms with the former but struggled with the latter. He agreed that what a person ate didn't make him clean or unclean before God and chose his meals that way—but only in certain circles.

Afraid to confront legalism, Peter acted hypocritically. There was a disconnect between what Peter taught and how he lived, and others were following his lead.

Out of love for the gospel and people, Paul confronted Peter. He reminded him that every single person who is justified (that is, made right) before God is justified by faith in Christ and nothing else—not circumcision, the dinner menu, or who he or she goes to dinner with.

The truth of his words didn't make the confrontation any less awkward. Peter was one of Jesus's original twelve disciples. Within that group, he was one of Jesus's three closest friends. He had a history as Paul did, but they were both found by the same Savior and the same gospel.

Paul was a relative newcomer, but that didn't stop him. His priority was the gospel. As such, he loved people enough to engage Peter in a difficult conversation. The truth was too important.

In Christ, Paul was free to rightly contend with Peter. He was not Peter's servant (Galatians 1:10); he was Jesus's servant, and Peter needed correction. The truth of the gospel was still at stake. Paul loved Peter enough to tell him to his face.

The gospel frees you to confront in love.

REFLECTIONS

Peter knew the gospel. He had preached it and led thousands to faith in Christ. Why, then, did Paul need to explain the gospel to him?

Describe a situation in which you have confidently exercised the freedom to contend for the gospel (or would).

Describe a situation in which you need to contend for the gospel but have held back in fear. How does Paul's example here encourage you in that?

CONNECTING THE STORY

In Acts 10, God gave Peter a vision to teach him Jesus's death on the cross surpassed and supplanted the necessity of the dietary laws. Immediately after, He gave Peter personal experience to confirm the vision's message, which Peter then embraced by eating with Gentiles. However, when Jews from Jerusalem were around, Peter went back to his old ways, choosing to not eat "unclean" foods or even share a meal with Gentiles.

GALATIANS 2:19-21

[19] For through the law I died to the law, so that I might live for God. [20] I have been crucified with Christ, and I no longer live, but Christ lives in me. The life I now live in the body, I live by faith in the Son of God, who loved me and gave himself for me. [21] I do not set aside the grace of God, for if righteousness comes through the law, then Christ died for nothing.

FOR LIFE

The gospel shows us two ways to live. One way involves rest and trust in God. It involves knowing He loves and accepts you through Jesus, no matter what you've done or ever will do for Him.

There's also another way that even true Christians get caught in—self effort. This way says ultimately we're made right by what we do, how we live, or "being a good person"—whatever that means. But what's the real difference between these two fundamental approaches to life?

Paul gives some insight into what makes the difference—a conscious decision to never set aside the grace of God.

Paul refused to turn back to a system of salvation through good effort. He tried it and found it lacking. That was the message he had been saved from. Paul died to that "gospel." He chose grace, instead. And in doing so, he chose *life*.

A choice that important was one he wouldn't only contend for himself. Paul, like Jesus, saw the people around Him and wanted better for them. He wanted to introduce them to the gospel that frees them from striving. He wanted them to see that Jesus accepts those weary from trying because His yoke is easy and His burden is light (Matthew 11:28-30). Paul determined to fight for them too.

After all, in choosing to follow Christ we put our old lives to death. And doing so brings us new life.

In this new life we get to experience the rest that comes from abiding in Jesus. As we live by faith in Jesus, the Holy Spirit within us accomplishes through us what we never could.

The life of faith is a life that holds onto grace. It's not up to human effort, ability, ingenuity, and will to experience abundant life (John 10:10). If it were, Jesus died for nothing, and we are hopeless. But in God's saving grace and redemptive love, we are made righteous and get to join His mission of bringing hope to a lost and dying world.

The life of faith holds on to grace.

What would it look like practically for you to live as someone who is "free to contend"?

What steps of faith and obedience is God asking you to take through these Scriptures?

PRAY

False teaching is just as dangerous for the church today as it was for the early church. Thank God for the truth of His Word and His Spirit who guides you in gospel partnership with believers from a variety of backgrounds. Ask Him to help you rightly contend for the pure gospel message.

WEEK 3

FREE TO CONTINUE

Faith grows in God's grace.

Jesus doesn't give us just enough grace to save us and then set us on our way to prove we are worth it.

That's the struggle, though, isn't it?

Every person who comes to faith in Christ does so recognizing salvation as a gift—completely unearned. There is, in fact, no other starting point for genuine faith. We acknowledge our need for salvation and trust in Jesus who died in our place.

But somewhere along the way, we begin to act as though the rest is up to us. We know we are saved by grace, but we think becoming Christlike depends on our own good efforts.

It doesn't. In fact, in Galatians 3, Paul calls that idea pure foolishness.

We are saved by the gospel of grace. We continue in grace through the work of the Spirit in us. And it is in this same grace that we will one day meet Jesus face-to-face.

GALATIANS 3:1-5

JUSTIFICATION THROUGH FAITH

3 You foolish Galatians! Who has cast a spell on you, before whose eyes Jesus Christ was publicly portrayed as crucified? [2] I only want to learn this from you: Did you receive the Spirit by the works of the law or by believing what you heard? [3] Are you so foolish? After beginning by the Spirit, are you now finishing by the flesh? [4] Did you experience so much for nothing — if in fact it was for nothing? [5] So then, does God give you the Spirit and work miracles among you by your doing the works of the law? Or is it by believing what you heard —

<table>
<tr><td>DAY
15</td><td></td></tr>
</table>

IN FAITH

If you know Jesus, think back to the moment that happened.

How did it happen? Did you become saved because you raised your hand or walked forward in a church service? Was it something you read? A prayer you repeated? Was it because someone dunked you under water or sprinkled your forehead?

This is the heart of Paul's line of questioning. He wanted the Galatians to see it clearly. They hadn't received the Spirit of God because they had performed any ritual—God poured out His grace and gave them His Spirit because they believed in Jesus.

That is the story of every person God has ever saved—Jesus plus nothing.

At the cross, Jesus completed the work of salvation for all who believe. He announced this when He gave up His spirit: "It is finished" (John 19:30). This finishing work involves the point we become Christians and every moment going forward. Jesus's work on the cross and resurrection empowers us as we continue to believe.

In other words, God doesn't give us His Spirit simply as a spectator to cheer our good works. He gives us His Spirit to initiate and produce those good works!

We don't begin the life of faith in grace and then continue through our best efforts. The way we live the Christian life is the same way we began it—by believing in the finished work of Jesus.

You live the Christian life the same way you began it.

REFLECTIONS

Put the Galatians' spiritual problem in your own words (vv. 3-4).

What do you feel like you have to do regularly to remain in good standing with God?

Why do you think we struggle to believe the gospel is not only sufficient for our salvation but also our spiritual growth? Why is this dangerous?

grow in
GRACE

The word *sanctification* refers to the process of being made holy and carries with it a certain result—a changed lifestyle. That certainty, though, comes through God's grace, not human effort. To live otherwise is to depart from faith altogether. Paul asked the Galatians, "Did you experience so much for nothing—if in fact it was for nothing?" (3:4). We receive the gift of the Spirit by grace through faith, and we continue in the gifts of the Spirit by His power at work in us. Read these verses from other New Testament passages that describe the Spirit's work in the process of every believer's sanctification.

The Spirit sets us apart to be cleansed by Christ's blood and to walk in obedience to Christ.

> Through the sanctifying work of the Spirit, to be obedient
> and to be sprinkled with the blood of Jesus Christ. **1 PETER 1:2**

The Spirit puts to death the power of our flesh and empowers us to walk in new life.

> Now if Christ is in you, the body is dead because of sin,
> but the Spirit gives life because of righteousness. **ROMANS 8:9-13**

The Spirit continually transforms us into the image of Christ as we seek Him.

> We all, with unveiled faces, are looking as in a mirror at the glory of the Lord
> and are being transformed into the same image from glory to glory; this is from
> the Lord who is the Spirit. **2 CORINTHIANS 3:18**

The Spirit reveals the truth of God's Word to us.

> We have not received the spirit of the world, but the Spirit who comes from
> God, so that we may understand what has been freely given to us by God.
> **1 CORINTHIANS 2:6-16**

The Spirit produces His traits in us with outward effect.

> The fruit of the Spirit is love, joy, peace, patience, kindness, goodness,
> faithfulness, gentleness, and self-control. **GALATIANS 5:22-23**

The Spirit invites us to join Him in His sanctifying work and allows us the freedom
to make that choice.

> Don't stifle the Spirit. **1 THESSALONIANS 5:19**

GALATIANS 3:6-9

6 just like Abraham who believed God, and it was credited to him for righteousness?

[7] You know, then, that those who have faith, these are Abraham's sons. [8] Now the Scripture saw in advance that God would justify the Gentiles by faith and proclaimed the gospel ahead of time to Abraham, saying, All the nations will be blessed through you. [9] Consequently, those who have faith are blessed with Abraham, who had faith.

LETTING GO

It's hard to break away from long-standing traditions.

The Judaizers weren't trying to establish a new way of relating to God—they were struggling to break away from an old one. By the time Paul wrote Galatians, the law of Moses had existed for about fifteen hundred years. And they didn't want to let go.

Paul used their argument to make the point. The Judaizers wanted to talk about Moses, so Paul took them back 430 years further to Abraham. The first Hebrew patriarch and long-admired example of faith lived long before the Mosaic law was given, and he was declared righteous—not because of a diet or circumcision, but because of belief (Genesis 15:6).

Not only that, but Abraham's belief also impacted his life as it continued on earth. At the ages of one hundred and ninety respectively, God gave Abraham and his wife Sarah a son. They were long past childbearing years, which again proves the priority of God's grace over human prerogative and ability. Their son, Isaac, began the line of descendants that brought Jesus into the world.

The inclination to lean into the tradition of human effort as a way of earning God's favor now reaches forward nearly two thousand years after Paul's letter to the Galatians. And the message to us is the same.

We need to let go and lean into grace.

We are not saved by our participation in church, making the right decisions, reading our Bible, or anything we do in our religious lives. We are saved by grace alone.

God's plan of redemption didn't start with the law. It began with God's covenant promise. God's covenant promise extends to every person who has faith in Jesus. And it is God's covenant promise that carries our salvation into eternity.

Lean into grace.

REFLECTIONS

How does Abraham help us see the way of salvation and growth with God is not different between the Old Testament and New Testament? Does this surprise you?

Why is faith the necessary foundation for access to God's blessing?

What standards do you tend to add for people to have access to God? What needs to change?

INSIGHTS

God intended to save Gentiles all along—even in Old Testament times when He identified Jews as His chosen people. To express this, Paul quoted God's covenant with Abraham (Genesis 12:3), revealing God's heart for all nations from the very beginning. God blesses Abraham's *spiritual* descendants. God only blesses the physical descendants of Abraham who believe in Jesus. We are justified through faith, not bloodline or ritual.

GALATIANS 3:10-14

LAW AND PROMISE

¹0 For all who rely on the works of the law are under a curse, because it is written, Everyone who does not do everything written in the book of the law is cursed. 11 Now it is clear that no one is justified before God by the law, because the righteous will live by faith. 12 But the law is not based on faith; instead, the one who does these things will live by them. 13 Christ redeemed us from the curse of the law by becoming a curse for us, because it is written, Cursed is everyone who is hung on a tree. 14 The purpose was that the blessing of Abraham would come to the Gentiles by Christ Jesus, so that we could receive the promised Spirit through faith.

DAY 17

UNCURSED

Believing that God's love distorts our view of ourselves. Sometimes doing good works makes us think we deserve salvation, but not doing good works makes us think we can never receive salvation. And both attitudes keep us from experiencing from God's love.

If we rely on works, we're cursed if we do and cursed if we don't.

In fact, under the Mosaic law, any person who broke any part of any rule was cursed (Deuteronomy 27:26). That was the point of having 613 Old Testament commands—no one can keep the law perfectly. No one is deserving of salvation. Everyone is cursed. In Ephesians 2:1, Paul said it a different way: "You were dead in your trespasses and sins."

It's an important distinction. We tend to think our small sins get us a little bit off track with God. We concede our big sins are "pretty bad." But Paul teaches us this thinking undercuts the message of the gospel.

We're not a little bit off track in our sin. We're cursed. Our neighbors, coworkers, and friends aren't pretty bad off without Jesus, they're dead.

But "the righteous will live by faith" (Galatians 3:11).

Jesus took our curse on Himself at the cross. He died in our place. And all who trust in His work instead of their own will live with Him forever.

Believing we can earn God's love gives us a wrong view of self, but faith allows us to see ourselves rightly. The curse of death has been broken—we are redeemed in His gift of grace.

Jesus took your curse.

REFLECTIONS

Does Paul's description of people who don't do everything exactly right surprise you? Have you ever considered yourself as cursed because of sin?

Read Ephesians 2:1. Why do you think we tend to minimize the seriousness of sin?

What problems arise when we minimize the seriousness of sin? Is it possible to walk in freedom if we fail to identify ourselves as cursed and dead in sin?

GALATIANS 3:15-18

[15] Brothers and sisters, I'm using a human illustration. No one sets aside or makes additions to a validated human will. [16] Now the promises were spoken to Abraham and to his seed. He does not say "and to seeds," as though referring to many, but referring to one, and to your seed, who is Christ. [17] My point is this: The law, which came 430 years later, does not invalidate a covenant previously established by God and thus cancel the promise. [18] For if the inheritance is based on the law, it is no longer based on the promise; but God has graciously given it to Abraham through the promise.

UNDER GOD'S PROMISE

People break promises all the time. Campaign speeches are filled with "I will" statements that are later explained as, "I couldn't." Wedding ceremonies include promises of "I do" that sometimes change to "I didn't" or "I won't." In a world where it seems we break vows more often than we keep them, it can feel nearly impossible to believe anything or anyone is unchangeable.

But that's exactly who God is. When God told Abraham, "I will," He made a different kind of promise than those we encounter in our earthly experience. He is immutable—unchanging, and so is His Word. He is a covenant keeper. He is forever true to His character.

And His promise of salvation by faith to Abraham extends to every believer in Jesus Christ—permanently.

No alternate decision would then or will ever be made. No law could ever be written to nullify God's promise. The Mosaic law wasn't given to overturn the promise— that's impossible. It was given to show us our desperate need to *rely on* the promise.

People break their vows. That's why the promise was made! God's gift of salvation doesn't depend on human goodness—it counts on His own.

This means we have the freedom to entirely, always, and only depend on Jesus. We are saved by grace through faith, and we continue by grace through faith—not the works of the law.

God's promise cannot be undone.

God's promise to you will never be broken.

REFLECTIONS

What was Abraham's inheritance (and now yours) based on?

Why can't the law invalidate God's promise?

Why do you think it is so difficult for people to believe they cannot void God's promise?

INSIGHTS

Numbers 23:19 assures us, "God is not a man, that he might lie, or a son of man, that he might change his mind. Does he speak and not act, or promise and not fulfill?" However, some of us struggle to reconcile this with the places in Scripture where God seems to change His course of action (Exodus 32:7-14; Jeremiah 26:2-6; Jonah 3:10). These events do not contradict God's immutability, though. When God relents, He always does so according to His unchanging character and promise, not our action. Salvation by grace through faith is evident throughout the whole of Scripture. God relents when we repent.

GALATIANS 3:19-25

THE PURPOSE OF THE LAW

[19] Why, then, was the law given? It was added for the sake of transgressions until the Seed to whom the promise was made would come. The law was put into effect through angels by means of a mediator. [20] Now a mediator is not just for one person alone, but God is one. [21] Is the law therefore contrary to God's promises? Absolutely not! For if the law had been granted with the ability to give life, then righteousness would certainly be on the basis of the law. [22] But the Scripture imprisoned everything under sin's power, so that the promise might be given on the basis of faith in Jesus Christ to those who believe. [23] Before this faith came, we were confined under the law, imprisoned until the coming faith was revealed. [24] The law, then, was our guardian until Christ, so that we could be justified by faith. [25] But since that faith has come, we are no longer under a guardian,

DAY 19 | WITH CLARITY

The Galatians came by their confusion honestly. After all, the Bible is filled with commands. It can be difficult to reconcile the instruction to follow all those rules with the gospel of grace.

God didn't give the law to confuse us, though; He gave it to make our path forward crystal clear.

The commandments and Jesus's gift of grace work together for our eternal good. Without grace, we would be hopelessly confined and imprisoned (v. 23)—because we cannot break free from sin's power. And without the law, we wouldn't understand that we are confined and imprisoned in the first place.

So God gave us the law to act as a guardian or tutor—and not the kind who ignores mistakes to operate solely from a place of positive reinforcement. Under the teaching of the law, we lived with a constant awareness of wrongdoing and the threat of punishment.

Unlike grace, though, the law was temporary. It had both a starting point and an ending point. It came to Israel on Mount Sinai after the exodus, and it ended with Jesus's earthly advent.

In essence, the law set up the work Jesus came to do on the cross. Jesus fulfilled the law in His life, death, and resurrection.

Today, we are just as prone toward confusion as the Galatians. We struggle to reconcile God's commands with His gift of grace. And as Paul explains, it doesn't have to be that way.

The law's purpose was never to save. It was to clarify the freedom Christ came to give so that we might receive His grace and freely continue in it by faith.

God gave the law to make your
path forward crystal clear.

REFLECTIONS

In your own words, what is the purpose of the law?

How have you struggled to reconcile God's commands with His gift of grace in Jesus?

Are you more tempted to ignore the law or to ignore grace? What danger is there for you in that temptation?

PAUSE & LISTEN

Spend some time reflecting on the week's reading.

Are you so foolish?
After beginning by the Spirit,
are you now finishing by the flesh?

GALATIANS 3:3

REFLECTION

Use these questions for personal reflection or group discussion on Galatians 3:1-25.

What stuck out to you most in this week's reading? What surprised you? Confused you?

What does this week's Scripture teach you about God and His character?

What does this week's Scripture teach you about humanity and our need for grace?

What would it look like practically for you to live as someone who is "free to continue"?

What steps of faith and obedience is God asking you to take through these Scriptures?

PRAY

Thank God for His continuing grace, which empowers you to grow in righteousness. Confess your foolish tendency to lean into your own good efforts to become a person who is worthy of eternal life. Invite Him to show you those self-made paths and to lead you to fully embrace the work of His Spirit in you instead.

WEEK 4

FREE TO
IDENTIFY

Jesus makes us God's children.

If you had to pick one word to define who you are, what word would you choose? Would you choose a word that describes your profession? Your role in your family? A personality trait? A social or ethnic identifier? A political party?

In our increasingly polarizing world, it is easy to define ourselves by a group, person, or idea we oppose. Add to that the insatiable desire to explore the inner workings of our human psyche, and the nature to divide is evident. We don't click on a quiz asking, "Which superhero are you?" because we want to save the world. We take that quiz and others like it so that we might place ourselves in boxes that help us understand ourselves.

The early church had a similar inclination. There were different groups, distinctions, and methods, but the basic human tendency to divide was the same.

What Paul explains in Galatians is that, in Christ, we should see ourselves and other people through a different lens.

Jesus is our true identifier, and that should take a load off—both in how we view ourselves and how we view other people. In fact, it is only in Christ that we can ever truly and uniquely understand ourselves and freely relate to God and other people.

GALATIANS 3:26-29

[26] for through faith you are all sons of God in Christ Jesus.

SONS AND HEIRS

[27] For those of you who were baptized into Christ have been clothed with Christ.

[28] There is no Jew or Greek, slave or free, male and female; since you are all one in Christ Jesus. [29] And if you belong to Christ, then you are Abraham's seed, heirs

DAY
22

AS ONE

Have you ever shown up to an event and realized you were underdressed? Or maybe you've had the opposite experience where you dressed more formally and everyone else was in casual attire. Either way, that kind of experience can quickly make you feel like an outsider.

We often compare ourselves to others, especially based on the differences we can see. It can make us feel like we don't belong. But when we're in relationship with Christ, a sense of belonging always exists.

In Christ, God clothes us with an identity that supersedes every other factor and comparison. In Christ, we are each members of God's household.

We are His children and heirs of all He has promised. This is true no matter our race, economic status, gender, or any other factor that might otherwise divide us. That doesn't mean those aspects of our being are irrelevant, but they aren't primary. Jesus changes every person who trusts in Him from the inside out. We are clothed in Him and through Him, and all our differences become pieces of our testimony instead of points of disagreement.

The equality we have in Christ supersedes any division. He has made us one. He has broken down every barrier, unifying us for the advancement of His gospel of grace. We are free to lay down and put aside lesser differences to embrace our common hope in Christ.

There are no outsiders in God's family. There are no superiors or inferiors. Clothed in Christ, we are all equal. We are all welcome.

In Christ, you belong.

REFLECTIONS

What allegiances was Paul confronting in Galatians 3:28-29? Why?

How does seeing yourself as a Christian first change the way you see others?

What things shape your identity? How should the truth of Galatians 3:28 affect your understanding of who God is? Of who you are?

GALATIANS 4:1-7

4 according to the promise. [1] Now I say that as long as the heir is a child, he differs in no way from a slave, though he is the owner of everything. [2] Instead, he is under guardians and trustees until the time set by his father. [3] In the same way we also, when we were children, were in slavery under the elements of the world. [4] When the time came to completion, God sent his Son, born of a woman, born under the law, [5] to redeem those under the law, so that we might receive adoption as sons. [6] And because you are sons, God sent the Spirit of his Son into our hearts, crying, "*Abba*, Father!" [7] So you are no longer a slave but a son, and if a son, then God has made you an heir.

AS ADOPTED CHILDREN

Some rules we are forced to follow out of duty, all the while wondering why. We might think of a speed limit sign on an empty road in this way. We feel personally removed from the need to follow that law.

Other rules we want to follow from the heart—a properly buckled infant seat in that car, for example. We feel connected to the need to follow that law personally.

The difference between those two perspectives helps us understand Paul's meaning between slave and child in Galatians 4. The Mosaic law could compel duty, but it did not have the power to change our hearts. Under the law our hearts were still enslaved to sin and disconnected from God. But because God loves us, He wanted to free us by making us sons and daughters who *want* to obey. God sent Jesus to redeem us "when the time came to completion"—or in other words, at exactly the right time. Now we have the freedom to obey.

Everything that has ever happened in the world, and everything still to happen in the world, finds its center in the birth, death, and resurrection of Jesus Christ. He is the point of climax in the story of the world—in your own story and the story of every other person who has ever existed.

Through Christ's death and resurrection, we are adopted into God's family and are transformed from the inside out through our relationship with Him.

We no longer live as slaves, dutiful to a law we'd rather escape. In Jesus, we are changed by His Spirit to live as God's children—free to obey Him out of love rather than obligation.

The Spirit changes you to live as God's child.

REFLECTIONS

What does the idea that Jesus came into the world at exactly the right time communicate to you about God's plan? About His character?

Have you ever struggled to accept that you are a chosen and adopted child of God? Why do you think that is?

How does knowing you are God's child affect the way you approach obedience to Him?

INSIGHTS

Abba is the Aramaic word for "father." Jesus used it to speak of His intimate relationship with God (Mark 14:36; Luke 11:1-2). The word was often used in New Testament times, and well-known to the Galatians. In our day, we can correctly translate it as "daddy." God loves us as His children, and He invites us to love Him and treat Him as our Father.[1]

1. Adapted from Max Anders, *Galatians-Colossians*, vol. 8, Holman New Testament Commentary (Nashville, TN: Broadman & Holman Publishers, 1999), 56.

GALATIANS 4:8-11

PAUL'S CONCERN FOR THE GALATIANS

[8] But in the past, since you didn't know God, you were enslaved to things that by nature are not gods. [9] But now, since you know God, or rather have become known by God, how can you turn back again to the weak and worthless elements? Do you want to be enslaved to them all over again? [10] You are observing special days, months, seasons, and years. [11] I am fearful for you, that perhaps my labor for you has been wasted.

AS BEING KNOWN

Many of us struggle with the issue of identity because we feel trapped. We see ourselves in light of our past experiences, present circumstances, and future dreams. These are the measures we know and by which we become known.

Paul takes those trappings of earth a step further and explains that we are enslaved by them. We were created by God for God, but sin distorts that relationship, and we become bound to weak and worthless things.

The good news of the gospel of grace is that God shows us the way to freedom.

In Christ, we find what our hearts are so desperately looking for—to know God and to be known by Him, fully restored.

In Christ, our past experiences, present circumstances, and future dreams take on eternal meaning.

In Christ, the weak and worthless identities that previously enslaved us are replaced with His power and righteousness.

God knows everything about us. He knows our faults, our fears, our failures, and even our future. He makes us His children and invites us to walk in the freedom that relationship brings.

And Paul asks each of us an excellent question: Do you really want to turn back to those worthless identities and be trapped all over again?

God shows you the way to freedom, and He gives you a choice. You can live in the trappings of being known for the things you've done, the things you do, and the things you hope to do one day. Or, you can walk in the freedom that comes from being known by God because of the grace of Jesus.

You are known by God.

REFLECTIONS

How did Paul contrast the Galatians' lives before believing in Jesus and their lives after becoming Christians?

What was Paul asking in his rhetorical questions in verse 9? What are some "weak and worthless elements" you are tempted to turn back to? Why?

How can you avoid slipping back into the trappings of finding your identity in the things of this world?

INSIGHTS

The Galatian believers were Gentiles. As such, they had never been under slavery to the law of Moses. But they were in danger of becoming enslaved if they placed themselves under the law. In every culture and context, that temptation exists. In every culture and context, such a decision is weak and worthless because the law cannot bring righteousness or provide eternal life.

GALATIANS 4:12-20

[12] I beg you, brothers and sisters: Become as I am, for I also have become as you are. You have not wronged me; [13] you know that previously I preached the gospel to you because of a weakness of the flesh. [14] You did not despise or reject me though my physical condition was a trial for you. On the contrary, you received me as an angel of God, as Christ Jesus himself.

[15] Where, then, is your blessing? For I testify to you that, if possible, you would have torn out your eyes and given them to me. [16] So then, have I become your enemy because I told you the truth? [17] They court you eagerly, but not for good. They want to exclude you from me, so that you would pursue them. [18] But it is always good to be pursued in a good manner — and not just when I am with you. [19] My children, I am again suffering labor pains for you until Christ is formed in you. [20] I would like to be with you right now and change my tone of voice, because I don't know what to do about you.

AS ACCOUNTABLE

Conditional relationships make it difficult to thrive. If your relationships come with rules and requirements they feel forced rather than natural. They are legalistic, fickle, and constraining.

But relationships founded on grace are not fickle at all. Our relationship with God and with other Christians should be grace filled and freeing because they depend on the never-changing truth of God's Word and the unity we receive in Jesus. So even when conflict requires difficult conversations, relationships flourish.

Legalistic expectations divide and ultimately destroy relationships. Jesus's grace brings us together and holds us together as we grow together (Ephesians 4:16).

This is why Paul spoke so candidly to the Galatians. He wasn't wanting them to be accountable to him out of personal pride in his position. His motive was not self-focused at all. Paul wanted the Galatian believers to be accountable to the truth of God's Word. He was an instrument of sanctification God sovereignly placed in their lives—not because he was anything in and of himself but because he taught them the truth of grace. This is the kind of relationship Paul urged the Galatians to have and to pursue. He wanted them to be free as he was.

All of us lose sight of God's grace sometimes. To receive loving correction from other believers in those moments is healthy. To turn away from correction—even viewing those who offer it as enemies—is unhealthy (Galatians 4:16).

We are accountable to the gospel message. As such, we also must be accountable to each other. God has joined us together for the purpose of continuous growth.

God has joined you together with
other Christians to grow.

REFLECTIONS

Why was it so painful for Paul that the Galatian believers were abandoning what he taught them?

Contrast the false teachers' relational tact with Paul's (vv. 16-20). Which tact is more comfortable? Which tact is good and right?

How can you develop deeper levels of accountability in your relationships with God and others?

INSIGHTS

When Paul told the Galatians he had become as he was because he had become as they are, he meant that he, a Jew, had become like a Gentile. He was living with freedom from the restriction and requirements of the Jewish law. If he, a Jew, was free, he was puzzled as to why Gentile Christians would seek to make themselves like law-observing Jews.

GALATIANS 4:21-31

SARAH AND HAGAR: TWO COVENANTS

[21] Tell me, you who want to be under the law, don't you hear the law? [22] For it is written that Abraham had two sons, one by a slave and the other by a free woman. [23] But the one by the slave was born as a result of the flesh, while the one by the free woman was born through promise. [24] These things are being taken figuratively, for the women represent two covenants. One is from Mount Sinai and bears children into slavery — this is Hagar. [25] Now Hagar represents Mount Sinai in Arabia and corresponds to the present Jerusalem, for she is in slavery with her children. [26] But the Jerusalem above is free, and she is our mother. [27] For it is written,

> Rejoice, childless woman,
>
> unable to give birth.
>
> Burst into song and shout,
>
> you who are not in labor,
>
> for the children of the desolate woman will be many,
>
> more numerous than those
>
> of the woman who has a husband.

[28] Now you too, brothers and sisters, like Isaac, are children of promise. [29] But just as then the child born as a result of the flesh persecuted the one born as a result of the Spirit, so also now. [30] But what does the Scripture say? "Drive out the slave and her son, for the son of the slave will never be a coheir with the son of the free woman." [31] Therefore, brothers and sisters, we are not children of a slave but of the free woman.

DAY 26 AS THOSE WHO ARE FREE

A popular question used in groups as an icebreaker is, "If you could have a super power, what would it be?" We like to imagine ourselves with abilities beyond the human experience—super strength, teleportation, invisibility, flight, shapeshifting, or immortality—we could really get some things done!

As nice as it may be to imagine such extraordinary feats, though, they are pure fiction. The reality is, you can't save yourself or anyone else.

This was Paul's point in asking, "You who want to be under the law, don't you hear the law?" Every human attempt to do what only God can do only ends up making you a slave. If we place our identities in our abilities, whether real or imagined, we can never be God's children who are forever free.

Only God can bring about the fulfillment of God's promise.

Take Sarah and Hagar, for instance. Hagar was a slave, and her son Ishmael was born in the natural way of the flesh. His fleshly birth brought him into slavery too. Sarah, though, was free, and her son Isaac was born miraculously—his life was a clear fulfillment of God's promise. And his Spirit-produced birth brought him into God's family.

The allegory points to identity.

Hagar and Ishmael serve as a representation of our own need for extraordinary intervention. Our human abilities—our flesh—is the problem. Our only hope is to look to Christ and the salvation He provides. In Him, we are the children of the promise. We are not trapped in the slavery of our deficient abilities; we are God's children, forever freed by the all-sufficient power of His Spirit.

God frees you by the power of His Spirit.

REFLECTIONS

Restate Paul's question (v. 21) in your own words.

What does it mean that "the son of the slave will never be a coheir with the son of the free woman" (v. 30)?

Based on today's passage, how would you describe your identity?

INSIGHTS

Isaac was subject to Ishmael's persecution (Genesis 21:9-10), and Christians today will be subject to persecution from those whose identity is also found in *doing*. But an identity of *doing* never has the authority or blessing of God. We must choose to be free and act on that choice by ridding ourselves of such influences.

Know your
IDENTITY

An allegory is a spiritual or symbolic interpretation of a story that also has a literal meaning. In Galatians 4:21-31 Paul uses allegory to present the truth about Christian identity—we are children of promise. Consider what these other Bible passages that use allegory and metaphor teach us about our identity in Christ.

You are a new creation.

2 CORINTHIANS 5:17

You are God's temple.

1 CORINTHIANS 6:19-20

You are loved and forgiven by your Father.

LUKE 15:11-32

You are good soil, producing a good crop.

MATTHEW 13:3-9

You are the bride of Christ.

EPHESIANS 5:31-32

You are wholly dependent on Christ.

JOHN 15:1-8

You are a conqueror.

ROMANS 8:37

You are the light of the world.

MATTHEW 5:14-16

PAUSE & LISTEN

Spend some time reflecting on the week's reading.

When the time came to completion, God sent his Son, born of a woman, born under the law, to redeem those under the law, so that we might receive adoption as sons.

GALATIANS 4:4-5

REFLECTION

Use these questions for personal reflection or group discussion on Galatians 3:26–4:31.

What stuck out to you most in this week's reading? What surprised you? Confused you?

What does this week's Scripture teach you about God and His character?

What does this week's Scripture teach you about humanity and our need for grace?

What would it look like practically for you to live as someone who is "free to identify"?

In what way has your view of yourself shifted since beginning this study?

PRAY

Take some time to acknowledge your identity as God's child, fully known by Him and free to live in accountability and unity in grace with other believers. Thank Him for that gift.

FREE TO
BE FREE

Jesus has set us free.

Freedom means different things to different people.

A recent high school graduate thinks about newfound independence, hoping to do whatever he wants to do. A person in a toxic work environment longs for a new job where she can be free from unrealistic expectations. Parents look forward to seeing their children grow up to be who they are meant to be.

We readily identify the circumstantial constraints we long to be freed from, the experiences we want to be free to have, and the state of being we think we should be free to enjoy. Still, all these freedoms fall short of the freedom Jesus offers.

But what does it mean to be free in Jesus?

In Galatians 5, Paul helps us answer that important question. In fact, he begins the chapter with a bold proclamation. Christian freedom isn't a nebulous, faraway ideal—Jesus has already set us free.

This freedom, though, is different from our cultural ideals. Freedom in Christ isn't about doing whatever we want to do, it is about possessing the desire, power, and ability to do what God wants us to do. It's more about dependence than autonomy.

And according to Jesus, that's the only real freedom there is (John 8:36).

GALATIANS 5:1-6

FREEDOM OF THE CHRISTIAN

5 For freedom, Christ set us free. Stand firm, then, and don't submit again to a yoke of slavery. ² Take note! I, Paul, am telling you that if you get yourselves circumcised, Christ will not benefit you at all. ³ Again I testify to every man who gets himself circumcised that he is obligated to do the entire law. ⁴ You who are trying to be justified by the law are alienated from Christ; you have fallen from grace. ⁵ For we eagerly await through the Spirit, by faith, the hope of righteousness. ⁶ For in Christ Jesus neither circumcision nor uncircumcision accomplishes anything; what matters is faith working through love.

<table>
<tr><td>DAY
29</td><td># LOVING WHAT
GOD LOVES</td></tr>
</table>

LOVING WHAT GOD LOVES

God didn't send Jesus to die on the cross and rise from the grave to motivate us to seek His approval through our effort. In fact, living that kind of life has, ultimately, no benefit at all.

Jesus died on the cross and rose from the grave to set us free. His resurrection is the ultimate approval we need.

We can stand firm because of the freedom we have in Christ. Our footing is sure because our Savior is sure. We typically want to stand firm in our own determination, abilities, and efforts. But that stance always takes place in the context of slavery—*having* to follow God's commands, *needing* to tell people about Jesus, *obligated* to serve the church, *required* to love people, *trying* to show godly character. And the exhausting list goes on.

God positions our hearts differently as the gospel begins its work in our lives.

Instead of worrying that we are not enough or have not done enough, we eagerly wait in the security of grace, knowing we are receiving Jesus's righteousness as our own. Instead of having to be told to obey His commands, faith in Christ compels us to step into them willingly—because we love what God loves.

That change of heart frees us up to really live. We no longer have to be commanded to do what we love.

As we wait in the confidence of our final redemption, we have the freedom to *want* to do the things God wants us to do. In fact, we view it a joyful privilege that we *get* to. Faith in the grace of Christ shows itself in love.

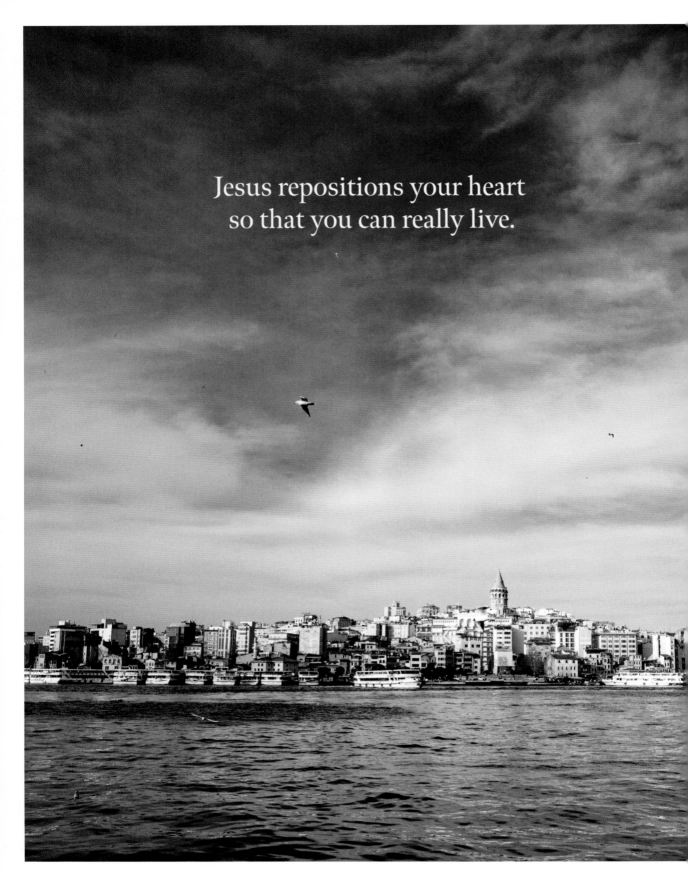

Jesus repositions your heart
so that you can really live.

REFLECTIONS

In your own words, what was Paul's warning in Galatians 5:1-6?

What is the only thing that matters as we "eagerly await ... the hope of righteousness" (v. 5)?

How should that fact change the way you live?

INSIGHTS

"Yoke"—a wooden frame placed on the backs of draft animals to make them pull in tandem—is used metaphorically in the Bible most often to speak of slavery, bondage, and hardship. In Galatians 5:1, Paul uses the word to explain that depending on the law for life and salvation makes work animals out of us. In Matthew 11:28-30, Jesus lets us know there is a better way—the way of grace. "Come to me, all of you who are weary and burdened, and I will give you rest. Take up my yoke and learn from me, because I am lowly and humble in heart, and you will find rest for your souls. For my yoke is easy and my burden is light."

GALATIANS 5:7-12

[7] You were running well. Who prevented you from being persuaded regarding the truth? [8] This persuasion does not come from the one who calls you. [9] A little leaven leavens the whole batch of dough. [10] I myself am persuaded in the Lord you will not accept any other view. But whoever it is that is confusing you will pay the penalty. [11] Now brothers and sisters, if I still preach circumcision, why am I still persecuted? In that case the offense of the cross has been abolished. [12] I wish those who are disturbing you might also let themselves be mutilated!

DAY
30

RUNNING WELL

To begin Galatians 5, Paul used the metaphor of a heavy yoke to describe the weight we carry when we depend on the law for salvation. Then he paints another word picture in verse 7 to continue this point—a race.

The Galatian believers needed to think back for a moment—they had been running well, but somewhere along the way they'd gotten tripped up.

It doesn't take much for that to happen.

To make that point, Paul switched again to a third metaphor—yeast in a ball of dough. Just a little bit of yeast (leaven) makes bread rise, and just a little bit of false teaching can wreck the whole person.

The same lesson can be taught numerous ways. As you're running the race God has set before you, another runner can accidentally or purposefully clip your heel. One errant foot from another runner can cause you to stumble. One divot or rock on the path can make you fall flat on your face.

False teaching is objectively disastrous for every Christian.

The Galatians had been running well, but then they encountered those wayward feet and deep divots and stray rocks. The obstacles didn't come from Christ, yet they held some kind of appeal.

We understand that appeal. We come to know Christ by grace through faith, and then along the way we find ourselves leaning into our good works. Expectations and opinions of others, whether expressed or perceived, trip us up.

It doesn't have to be that way.

Jesus is the truth that sets us free. His grace provides us freedom to run the race—and keep running well—free from the hurdles of burdens and expectations.

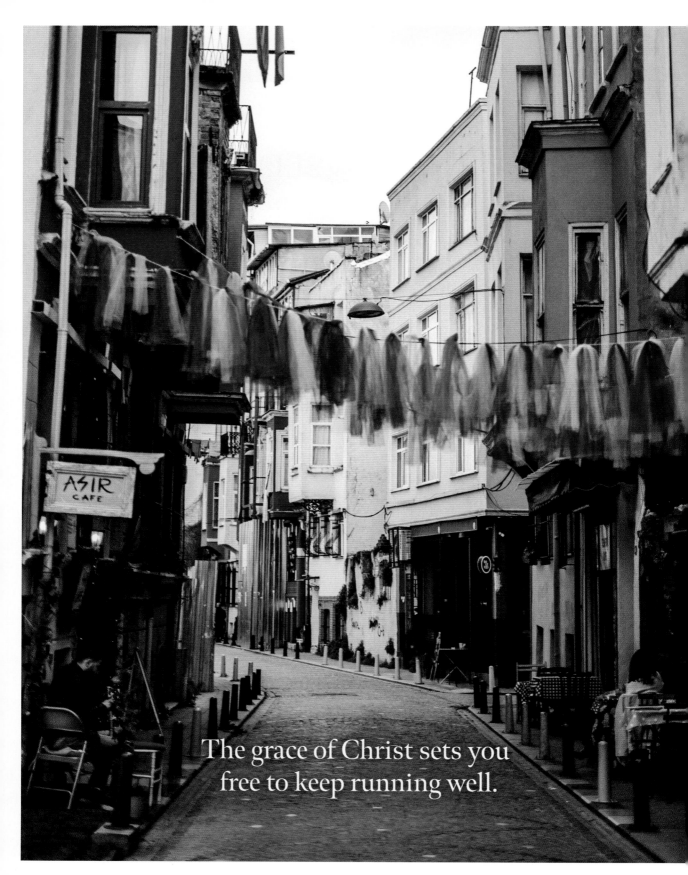

The grace of Christ sets you
free to keep running well.

REFLECTIONS

The Galatians started well, believing Paul's pure message about the gospel, and then chose to believe the legalistic message of the false teachers. How can you relate?

Specifically, what ideas, teachings, or cultural values and influences tend to trip you up?

How does living by grace alone free you to continue running well? Give an example.

GALATIANS 5:13-15

[13] For you were called to be free, brothers and sisters; only don't use this freedom as an opportunity for the flesh, but serve one another through love. [14] For the whole law is fulfilled in one statement: Love your neighbor as yourself. [15] But if you bite and devour one another, watch out, or you will be consumed by one another.

DAY 31 LOVING OTHER PEOPLE

When you were growing up, what chores did you have to do? You probably only did them because you had to, right? You lived under someone else's authority and you had to follow their rules. If you didn't do the chores you were assigned, you faced negative consequences. But once you become an adult and live in your own space, you have the freedom to choose for yourself whether or not you'll make your bed, wash the dishes, or take out the trash.

In the Old Testament, approaching God in worship was conditioned by the ceremonial law. Then Jesus came to change everything. We no longer relate to God in the same way we once did. Jesus's death and resurrection has removed the bondage of legalism and the weight of the law.

Christianity, then, isn't about following a list of rules. It's about freedom.

But we are tempted to twist that freedom.

That's why Paul cautions us to not take advantage of it. The freedom we have in Christ is not a pass to do whatever we want. It is not an impetus to serve ourselves. Rather, it is a compelling reason to love God with our whole heart, soul, mind, and strength—by loving and serving others as ourselves (Mark 12:30-31).

Love is the primary aim of the freedom Christ provides. In other words, We are freed to something, not *just* from something.

That objective is lost, though, when we judge ourselves and others according to a list of rules. When we choose to walk in that legalistic life Jesus helped us escape, we cause division and put everyone in the community of faith at risk of being consumed.

Jesus, though, offers a new life—abundant life. In Him, we know who we are and why. We know we have eternal life. We know we have holy purpose here on earth that perfectly aligns with the eternal life we will receive.

Left with nothing to prove, we are free to love and serve other people.

The grace of Christ frees you to love and serve other people.

REFLECTIONS

Christians are called to be free. What are some ways Christians might misunderstand or misuse that freedom?

What does love have to do with it? Why do you think Paul felt the need to include these words in Galatians 5:13?

What relationship or situation do you tend to approach more like verse 15 than verse 14? Why?

GALATIANS 5:16-18

THE SPIRIT VERSUS THE FLESH

[16] I say, then, walk by the Spirit and you will certainly not carry out the desire of the flesh. [17] For the flesh desires what is against the Spirit, and the Spirit desires what is against the flesh; these are opposed to each other, so that you don't do what you want. [18] But if you are led by the Spirit, you are not under the law.

DAY 32 | WALKING BY THE SPIRIT

God's instructions are simple. Galatians has encapsulated it this way so far: believe in Jesus, contend for grace, continue in faith, identify as God's child, and live in Christ's freedom. It should be easy, right? But more than a month into this study, you're likely reading Galatians 5:17 with a desire to shout your loudest "Amen!"

You're not alone. The struggle is real for every believer.

Opposing forces are at work within us. We want to please God, and at the very same time our sin nature leads us to think, say, and do things that displease Him. This is a battle we will face our entire earthly lives.

That's why verses 16 and 18 are so incredible—there is no law against the Spirit-led life. The grace of Jesus gives us freedom and life. The grace of the Spirit empowers us to continue in that freedom and life.

Yes, we face a continuing battle on this side of heaven. Yet because we know Jesus, sin no longer has the authority over us. Instead, we are free to submit our human will to the power of the Spirit who now indwells us.

Jesus freed us to walk in the power of His Spirit. He has given us the freedom not to sin.

Yes, there is a continual struggle in our lives here on earth, and there is also victory in that struggle. Our obedience to God's commands is empowered by God's Spirit. When we submit ourselves to Him moment by moment, He leads us to do what God wants, not what our sinful nature desires.

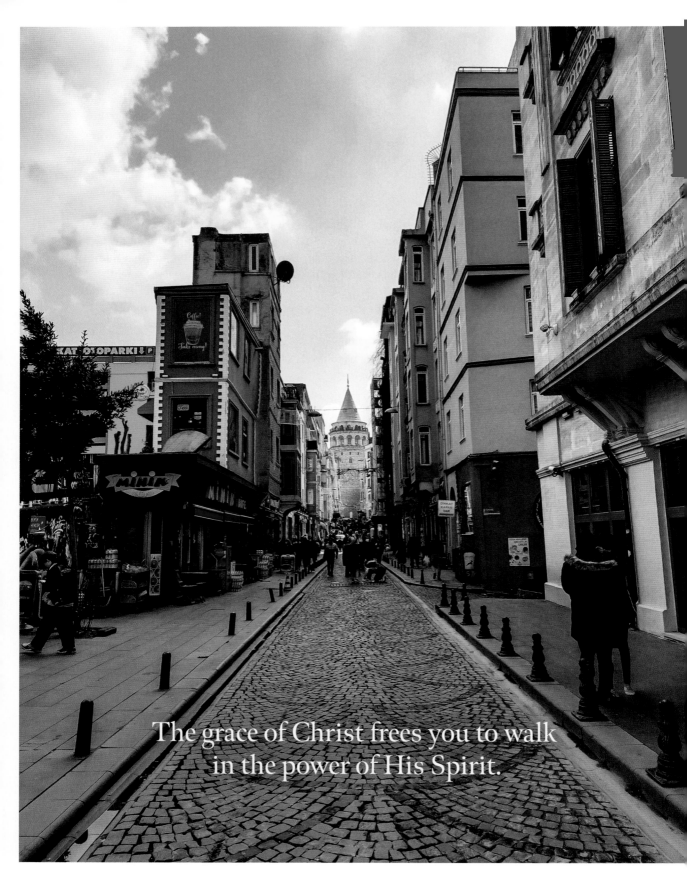

The grace of Christ frees you to walk
in the power of His Spirit.

REFLECTIONS

In your own words, what warning does Galatians 5:16-18 give?

In your own words, what encouragement do those verses give?

How does verse 17 play out in your daily life? What would it mean, practically, for you to walk by the Spirit as you face that struggle?

INSIGHTS

In Romans 7, Paul examines the battle between flesh and Spirit taking place in the life of every believer. He explains, "For I do not understand what I am doing, because I do not practice what I want to do, but I do what I hate" (v. 15). However, this is not a reason to justify sinful behavior. Instead, it is a reason to rejoice in the freedom of Christ: "What a wretched man I am! Who will rescue me from this body of death? Thanks be to God through Jesus Christ our Lord!" (vv. 24-25).

Walk in FREEDOM

Many of us come away from a study on Galatians 5 with a fresh resolve to be more patient, more kind, and to show more self-control. But that's not how we walk in the freedom of Christ. We are free to be free—loving what God loves, running well, loving other people, walking by the Spirit, and bearing fruit—when we begin to wholly rely on Jesus instead of ourselves.

Read John 15:1-11 to better understand what it truly means to walk in freedom.

JOHN 15:1-11

THE VINE AND THE BRANCHES

15 "I am the true vine, and my Father is the gardener. ² Every branch in me that does not produce fruit he removes, and he prunes every branch that produces fruit so that it will produce more fruit. ³ You are already clean because of the word I have spoken to you. ⁴ Remain in me, and I in you. Just as a branch is unable to produce fruit by itself unless it remains on the vine, neither can you unless you remain in me. ⁵ I am the vine; you are the branches. The one who remains in me and I in him produces much fruit, because you can do nothing without me. ⁶ If anyone does not remain in me, he is thrown aside like a branch and he withers. They gather them, throw them into the fire, and they are burned. ⁷ If you remain in me and my words remain in you, ask whatever you want and it will be done for you. ⁸ My Father is glorified by this: that you produce much fruit and prove to be my disciples.

CHRISTLIKE LOVE

⁹ "As the Father has loved me, I have also loved you. Remain in my love. ¹⁰ If you keep my commands you will remain in my love, just as I have kept my Father's commands and remain in his love. ¹¹ "I have told you these things so that my joy may be in you and your joy may be complete.

Galatians 5:1a

Galatians 5:7-8

Galatians 5:22

Galatians 5:21

Galatians 5:16, 25a

Galatians 5:18

GALATIANS 5:19-26

[19] Now the works of the flesh are obvious: sexual immorality, moral impurity, promiscuity, [20] idolatry, sorcery, hatreds, strife, jealousy, outbursts of anger, selfish ambitions, dissensions, factions, [21] envy, drunkenness, carousing, and anything similar. I am warning you about these things — as I warned you before — that those who practice such things will not inherit the kingdom of God.

[22] But the fruit of the Spirit is love, joy, peace, patience, kindness, goodness, faithfulness, [23] gentleness, and self-control. The law is not against such things. [24] Now those who belong to Christ Jesus have crucified the flesh with its passions and desires. [25] If we live by the Spirit, let us also keep in step with the Spirit. [26] Let us not become conceited, provoking one another, envying one another.

<table>
<tr><td>DAY
33</td><td># BEARING FRUIT</td></tr>
</table>

Most children go through a phase when they ask the question, "Why?" far more than adults would prefer. They're not trying to annoy us, though—they legitimately want to understand. Kids learn some things just by watching and observing the world, but we need to explain some things too.

In a way, we're all kind of like that, even as adults. We don't understand God's ways, and we need the Holy Spirit to reveal more of God to us. We don't understand why we should respond with love when people act in a way that makes them hard to even *like*. We wonder why in the world we should treat them with gentleness when everything in us believes we are justified in certain unkindnesses.

That's why we need God to work in us to shape us into the people He designed us to be.

And God's Word calls us to do just that—to follow the Spirit's leadership and avoid destructive attitudes and behavior. This isn't only for pastors and missionaries. It is for "those who belong to Christ" (v. 24). In other words, anyone who trusts in Jesus as Savior and Lord is meant to stop practicing the works of the flesh and start demonstrating the fruit of the Spirit.

We make this choice daily. In Jesus, we live by God's Spirit and keep in step with God's Spirit.

So when it comes down to it, why is far less important than how. We don't summon love, joy, peace, patience, and kindness out of our own good efforts. We can't force our hearts toward goodness, faithfulness, gentleness, and self-control.

Instead, the Spirit gives us the power we need to live out our faith.

As we remain connected to Him, He replaces the sinful works of our flesh with outworkings of His character. He destroys our old nature—instead of it destroying us.

The grace of Christ frees you
to live out your faith.

REFLECTIONS

Are you often aware of the Spirit's presence and power in your life? Why? How can you be more aware of and sensitive to the Spirit's presence and power?

Regarding the works of the flesh, Paul wrote "those who practice such things will not inherit the kingdom of God" (v. 21). This might seem contradictory to the message of grace given in Galatians. So, what does this verse mean? What does it not mean?

As you read the characteristics listed in Galatians 5:22-23, what "why" question do you come up against? Based on the whole passage, how can you overcome that struggle to keep in step with the Spirit?

For freedom, Christ set us free. Stand firm, then, and don't submit again to a yoke of slavery.

GALATIANS 5:1

REFLECTION
Use these questions for personal reflection or group discussion on Galatians 5.

What stuck out to you most in this week's reading? What surprised you? Confused you?

What does this week's Scripture teach you about God and His character?

What does this week's Scripture teach you about humanity and our need for grace?

What would it look like practically for you to live as someone who is "free to be free"?

How has another believer encouraged you to live in the freedom of Christ? How can you encourage someone to live in the freedom of Christ?

PRAY

Thank God for the Holy Spirit's presence in your life, guiding and advocating for you to live a life that glorifies God. Ask Him to help you keep in step with the Spirit.

WEEK 6

FREE TO DO GOOD

Jesus makes goodness
come to life.

When you read a book, you move from front to back. You might look at the last page before you get there, but you wouldn't start there and read backward. That would be disorienting. In the end, you would be no more aware of the truth of the story than when you first began.

The order of a story matters.

And the order by which we step into Christian freedom matters, too. It is not insignificant or surprising, then, that Paul began Galatians with the call to grace and ended his letter with the call to do good.

Grace is the starting place. The way we live is the end effect.

We, like the Galatians, are tempted to start from the place of good works. We think we can move forward from those good works to freedom in Jesus. And it disorients us, leaving us enslaved and entirely unfulfilled.

Faith is the springboard for life in Christ, and that faith is based on the grace of God, through the saving work of Jesus on the cross. It is then, and only then, that true goodness can come to life in us.

In light of the gospel of grace and the power of the Holy Spirit, we are made free to help others.

GALATIANS 6:1-2

CARRY ONE ANOTHER'S BURDENS

6 Brothers and sisters, if someone is overtaken in any wrongdoing, you who are spiritual, restore such a person with a gentle spirit, watching out for yourselves so that you also won't be tempted. ² Carry one another's burdens; in this way you will fulfill the law of Christ.

DAY 36

CARRYING BURDENS

Do Paul's first two sentences in Galatians 6 cause you some level of internal struggle?

Relationships need healthy boundaries, and it's not our job to fix other people, right? On top of that, we each have plenty of our own issues to deal with. So what exactly is God's Word instructing us to do here? To what extent are we responsible for other people? And what does it mean to restore a sinful person and to carry other people's burdens anyway?

To answer those questions, it's important to remember Paul's words in Galatians 5— for freedom, Christ set us free. And that freedom isn't self-serving; it compels us to serve one another in love.

When we're centered in the desires of the flesh, it's tough to have patience with people, notice their needs, or even care that they have those needs. That's because other people's concerns are the last thing on our minds.

Keeping in step with the Spirit, though, leads us to prioritize the concerns of others—because we understand that those issues impact *their* steps with the Spirit. And their steps with the Spirit should be marked by freedom, too.

It's true, healthy boundaries are important and it's not our job to fix other people. At the same time, we must interpret those truths in light of the freedom we have received in Christ.

Finding the right balance in relationships can be tricky, but one thing is clear: the Christian life is meant to be lived in community. God wants us to connect with other believers in meaningful ways—especially in times marked by sin and struggle. Christian freedom is not just about overcoming your challenges; it's about helping other people overcome theirs.

God wants you to connect with other believers in meaningful ways.

REFLECTIONS

What is your initial reaction to these verses?

Only when Jesus returns will our personal battle with sin be finished. Until that day, God has designed us to live together in community, strengthening and sharpening each other until that day (Proverbs 27:17). What would it look like for you to bear with other believers in this way?

Define healthy boundaries in light of God's call on your life to restore sinful people and carry burdens.

TRACING THE STORY

In Galatians 6:2, Paul referred to "the law of Christ." Matthew 22:37-40 helps us know what Paul likely meant by that. From the first pages of Scripture to the last, all of them are interconnected toward this command—love God and people. Paul's instruction in Galatians 6, then, lets us know in plain language that loving people involves carrying their burdens.

GALATIANS 6:3-5

[3] For if anyone considers himself to be something when he is nothing, he deceives himself. [4] Let each person examine his own work, and then he can take pride in himself alone, and not compare himself with someone else. [5] For each person will have to carry his own load.

UNDECEIVED

Sometimes carrying other people's burdens feels like a *have to*—and that's no good.

Have to isn't synonymous with freedom. Walking in Christ's freedom should be marked by *get tos*. Not only that, but the difference between *have to* and *get to* impacts the whole community of faith. That's why Paul continued his teaching with a deep dive, all the way down to our motives.

It is possible to do something good for a bad reason. And, whether we like it or not, motives matter.

When we relate to one another because we think we *have to*, we revert to a works-based system of belief. A works-based system of belief deceives us and turns our hearts and minds toward comparison. Comparison then turns to pride and, before you know it, the burdens we carry become heavier and heavier for everyone involved.

To that point, verses 3-5 give us a warning: If you think you're above failing like another person, you are deceiving yourself. If you think you would never experience a circumstance that would be so heavy you'd need help carrying its weight, you're wrong. You will, in fact, have to carry your own load.

The way to carry burdens, then, starts with the motive of grace.

In the grace of Jesus Christ, we have no reason to compare or entertain prideful thoughts. Instead, grace clears our vision to reject any standard besides the Scriptures and the life of His Spirit dwelling in us.

So before we get an inflated sense of self-importance about all the burden bearing we *have to* do, let's join Paul in that deep dive. Let's invite the Holy Spirit to reveal and address any deception inside us. When we do, we will better understand just how incredible the grace we have received really is, and we will see carrying burdens as a *get to*.

God wants you to investigate your motives.

REFLECTIONS

From Paul's words here, what practice helps keep you from comparing yourself to others?

Why is comparison so much more common than spiritual self-examination?

In what ways are you tempted to compare yourself to others? What are some steps you can take to avoid doing so?

GALATIANS 6:6-10

[6] Let the one who is taught the word share all his good things with the teacher. [7] Don't be deceived: God is not mocked. For whatever a person sows he will also reap, [8] because the one who sows to his flesh will reap destruction from the flesh, but the one who sows to the Spirit will reap eternal life from the Spirit. [9] Let us not get tired of doing good, for we will reap at the proper time if we don't give up. [10] Therefore, as we have opportunity, let us work for the good of all, especially for those who belong to the household of faith.

DAY 38

REAPING WHAT WE SOW

When have you started something new, feeling full of excitement, energy, and purpose, only to lose steam halfway through? Sometimes we start drifting from our goals and plans, and we don't even realize it's happening. Maybe the work was harder than we imagined. Maybe unexpected obstacles popped up.

Carrying burdens can be that way. We sometimes step into a need with the right motive, only to soon find ourselves viewing it as an unwelcome duty. But the call to do good isn't a onetime call—it is the lifestyle of following Jesus.

This isn't to say each burden we help carry comes with a lifetime membership! However, as we engage in a lifestyle of doing good, days and seasons will come when we get tired, growing weary of what we once knew was right and good. In those times, we might feel tempted to give up. We might get frustrated and take ourselves out of the doing for a while, thinking the hard work should be left to better Christians.

Sometimes we won't see the benefit of the work God calls us to. We won't know why we should share all good things or how we can keep working for the good of all people. In our earthly view, it won't make sense. And God asks us to look ahead and see the bigger picture.

In due time, we will reap what we sow.

Life has a way of making us weary, but God desires for us to keep doing good, and He will empower us for that work. So we can keep giving generously of our resources, our abilities, and ourselves. As we do, we can know the work will prove its worth in eternity.

God wants you to look ahead
and see the bigger picture.

REFLECTIONS

Considering the context, what did Paul mean by "God is not mocked" (v. 7)?

Practically speaking, what are some opportunities you have to keep doing good?

In what situations are you growing tired of doing good? How does today's passage encourage you?

DO GOOD
to Others

Galatians makes it clear that good deeds are not the starting place in relationship with God (Galatians 2:16). The starting place is the cross of Christ. At the same time, the gift of grace we receive in Christ impacts our deeds. Grace always manifests itself in loving actions, because that's the kind of life the Spirit empowers.

LOVE PEOPLE. Do everything in love. *1 Corinthians 16:14* **EVEN THE ONES WHO ARE HARD TO LIKE.** Love your enemies, do what is good, and lend, expecting nothing in return. *Luke 6:35* **NOTICE THEIR NEEDS** Everyone should look not to his own interests, but rather to the interests of others. *Philippians 2:4* **AND THEN STEP INTO THOSE NEEDS** If a brother or sister is without clothes and lacks daily food and one of you says to them, "Go in peace, stay warm, and be well fed," but you don't give them what the body needs, what good is it? *James 2:15-16* **BY BEING GENEROUS** Be generous and willing to share. *1 Timothy 6:18* **AND SHOWING MERCY.** Then Jesus told him, "Go and do the same." *Luke 10:37* **BE HONEST AND PRAY WITH OTHER PEOPLE ABOUT YOUR STRUGGLES.** Confess your sins to one another and pray for one another, so that you may be healed. *James 5:16* **AND FORGIVE THEM IN THEIRS.** And whenever you stand praying, if you have anything against anyone, forgive him. *Mark 11:25* **AS YOU DO THOSE GOOD WORKS, ENCOURAGE OTHER PEOPLE TO DO GOOD WORKS.** And let us consider one another in order to provoke love and good works. *Hebrews 10:24* **BY SAYING KIND, HELPFUL THINGS** No foul language should come from your mouth, but only what is good for building up someone in need, so that it gives grace to those who hear. *Ephesians 4:29* **AS THE LIGHT OF CHRIST SHINES THROUGH US** In the same way, let your light shine before others, so that they may see your good works and give glory to your Father in heaven. *Matthew 5:16* **THE WORLD WILL KNOW THAT WE BELONG TO HIM** By this everyone will know that you are my disciples, if you love one another. *John 13:35*

GALATIANS 6:11-13

CONCLUDING EXHORTATION

[11] Look at what large letters I use as I write to you in my own handwriting. [12] Those who want to make a good impression in the flesh are the ones who would compel you to be circumcised — but only to avoid being persecuted for the cross of Christ. [13] For even the circumcised don't keep the law themselves, and yet they want you to be circumcised in order to boast about your flesh.

WITH HUMILITY

Sometimes we confuse our pride for humility. For example, a well-meaning Christian might turn down an opportunity to speak into an important issue because he thinks he won't know what to say (see Exodus 4:10). Or maybe a person might be tempted to not give a financial gift because she doesn't think her small offering could possibly matter (see Mark 12:41-44).

The difference between pride and humility can be tricky to discern. But worrying about the way something looks to other people is a sure sign of pride.

Paul gave a personal example. What if he had decided not to write his letter to the Galatians, or any letter, for that matter, because his penmanship was awful? Would he have been right or wrong in making that decision?

Paul knew it would have been wrong, and he made that point clear in verse 11 by taking over the scribe's pen to write the concluding words with his own hand.

False teachers wanted to "make a good impression in the flesh" (v. 12). They cared more about how they looked to others than whether their ministry honored God. They also wanted to avoid persecution. The Jewish religion was accepted in the Roman Empire, but being a Christian could get you killed.

Paul's message? Their behavior was an effect of slavery, not freedom.

We might be tempted to brush past Paul's words here because we aren't false teachers. But their motives can consume us too. It is easy for us to get caught up in managing our image and pretending to be deeply spiritual when, in reality, we struggle.

But Jesus came to set us free from that struggle. We disguise our pride as humility, and it keeps us from admitting our fears and our needs. We don't want others to see our flaws. Trusting Christ, though, means being willing to let Him expose our vulnerabilities so that we can step fully into His calling on our lives to let Him empower us to do as much good as possible—for His glory, not ours.

Stepping fully into God's calling on your life to do good requires humility.

REFLECTIONS

What danger comes with being overly concerned with how your life or ministry appears to others?

In what specific way does pride cause you to struggle to do what God has called you to do?

What are we missing about God when we pretend that we have it all together?

INSIGHTS

Paul's explanation that false teachers preached circumcision "*only* to avoid being persecuted" (v. 12, emphasis added) might strike us as strange. However, Paul wasn't inferring that persecution is a small concern. Rather, he understood, as Jesus and the New Testament apostles taught and experienced, that persecution is an expected part of faith, which ultimately brings blessing (Matthew 5:10,44; 1 Peter 4:12-14; 1 John 3:13; 2 Corinthians 12:10).

GALATIANS 6:14-18

[14] But as for me, I will never boast about anything except the cross of our Lord Jesus Christ. The world has been crucified to me through the cross, and I to the world. [15] For both circumcision and uncircumcision mean nothing; what matters instead is a new creation. [16] May peace come to all those who follow this standard, and mercy even to the Israel of God!

[17] From now on, let no one cause me trouble, because I bear on my body the marks of Jesus. [18] Brothers and sisters, the grace of our Lord Jesus Christ be with your spirit. Amen.

BOASTING IN THE CROSS

In the 1991 movie *City Slickers*, a tough cowboy named Curly asks a salesman named Mitch, "Do you know what the secret of life is?" Mitch admits he doesn't know the secret of life, so Curly holds up his index finger and says "This. One thing. Just one thing." Mitch then asks what the one thing is, so Curly smiles and says, "That's what you've gotta figure out."[1]

It is with that same sort of confidence that Paul concluded his letter to the Galatians. In fact it is the theme of the entire book. Only one thing truly matters in life, only one thing is worth boasting about—the cross of our Lord Jesus Christ.

That's because, at the cross, Jesus makes us new creations. At the cross, we walk out of slavery and into freedom. At the cross, we receive abundant life (John 10:10).

We are all tempted to mistake the one thing that matters in life as our own good works. But nothing in our works is worth boasting about. In fact, the efforts of humanity are why Jesus went to the cross. Works only possess the power to keep us enslaved.

But by grace through faith in Jesus alone, we are saved.

Paul had come to embrace that truth in his life and the purpose of Galatians is for us to embrace it too.

You don't have to figure it out, and it's no secret anyway. Jesus has secured our salvation, and there is freedom for every person who embraces this one thing.

1. Ron Underwood, dir., *City Slickers* (Beverly Hills: Castle Rock Entertainment, 1991), DVD.

Only one thing matters.

REFLECTIONS

In your own words, what one thing mattered to Paul?

Why is boasting in our own abilities and good efforts pointless?

What might people who know you well say is the one thing that matters most to you? How does Galatians teach you about that?

PAUSE & LISTEN

Spend some time reflecting on the week's reading.

Carry one another's burdens; in this way you will fulfill the law of Christ.

GALATIANS 6:2

DAY
42

REFLECTION
Use these questions for personal reflection or group discussion on Galatians 6.

What stuck out to you most in this week's reading? What surprised you? Confused you?

What does this week's Scripture teach you about God and His character?

What does this week's Scripture teach you about humanity and our need for grace?

What would it look like practically for you to live as someone who is "free to do good"?

What good work is the grace of Christ now compelling you to do?

PRAY

Take some time to reflect on God's good work in your life. Invite Him to show you ways you can think and act to reflect that good work.

PHOTOGRAPHY CREDITS

FOUNDATIONS
NEW TESTAMENT
FOR BUSY BELIEVERS
BIBLE READING PLAN FOR GROUPS
FOUNDATIONS
OLD TESTAMENT
A 260-DAY BIBLE READING PLAN FOR BUSY BELIEVERS
ROBBY & KANDI GALLATY
REPLICATE

Manageable one-year plans for Bible reading

Foundations gives you a one-year Bible reading plan that requires just five days of study per week to fit your busy schedule. It includes daily devotional material. And through the HEAR journaling method, you'll learn how to Highlight, Explain, Apply, and Respond to passages, allowing for practical application.

Foundations
Study key passages of the Bible in one year,
while still having the flexibility of reading five days per week.

005769893 **$14.99**

Foundations: New Testament
Read and reflect on the New Testament in one year
with this reading and devotional guide.

005810327 **$14.99**

Foundations: Old Testament
Read through the story of the Old Testament in one year
using this manageable five-day-per-week plan.

005831469 **$14.99**

lifeway.com/foundations
Learn more online or call 800.458.2772.

To make a difference, you have to be different.

The book of Daniel is set in the heart of a hostile, pagan empire. Yet four Hebrew men found a way to honor God, and in doing so, participated in miraculous displays of God's glory. This new 8-session study of Daniel can help you and your men's group develop the courage, convictions, and habits of a faithful Christian. Perhaps God will use you to demonstrate His glory in today's Babylon.

Learn more online or call 800.458.2772.
lifeway.com/danielstudy

Lifeway

Step into God's beautiful story.

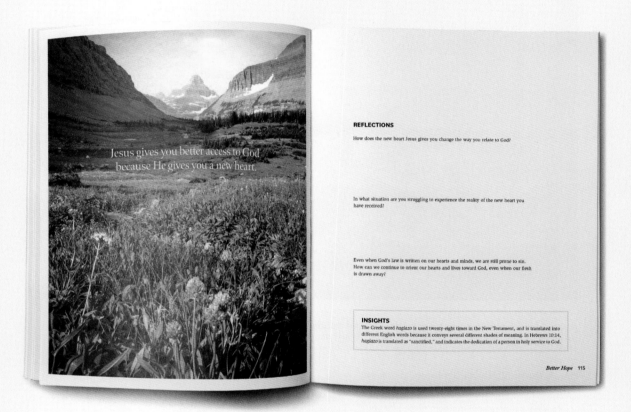

REFLECTIONS

How does the new heart Jesus gives you change the way you relate to God?

In what situation are you struggling to experience the reality of the new heart you have received?

Even when God's law is written on our hearts and minds, we are still prone to sin. How can we continue to orient our hearts and lives toward God, even when our flesh is drawn away?

INSIGHTS

The Greek word *hagiazo* is used twenty-eight times in the New Testament, and is translated into different English words because it conveys several different shades of meaning. In Hebrews 10:14, *hagiazo* is translated as "sanctified," and indicates the dedication of a person in holy service to God.

Better Hope 115

Storyteller is a Bible study series uniquely designed to be inviting, intuitive, and interactive. Each volume examines a key theme or story in a book of the Bible. Every week includes five days of short Scripture reading, a daily thought explaining each passage, a short list of questions for a group Bible study, and space for you to write down your discoveries. And new volumes are being added every year.

Learn more online or call 800.458.2772.
lifeway.com/storyteller

You are fully loved.

When you accepted Christ, you became a child of God. It's time to let go of unhealthy spiritual attitudes and rhythms that have been keeping you from the blessings of the gospel that Jesus died to give you.

As a believer, the freedom you have in Christ is not the absence of constraint or a license to live however you want. It is a deep and abiding commitment to love and serve others the way God intended for you.

This six-session Bible study is designed to help you:

- Understand the Christian definition of freedom
- Reassess what gospel freedom means for you
- See that there is no other gospel than the one Jesus offers
- Be encouraged to bear and share the burdens of others within the family of God

ADDITIONAL RESOURCES

eBOOK
Includes the content of this printed book but offers the convenience and flexibility that come with mobile technology.

005842045 **$19.99**

Storyteller resources and additional Bible study titles can be found online at lifeway.com/storyteller

Price and availability subject to change without notice.